T0133585

Lean Implementation in Hospital Departments

How to Move from Good to Great Services

By
A. Heri Iswanto

Routledge
Taylor & Francis Group

A PRODUCTIVITY PRESS BOOK

First edition published in 2019
by Routledge/Productivity Press
52 Vanderbilt Avenue, 11th Floor New York, NY 10017
2 Park Square, Milton Park, Abingdon, Oxon OX14 4RN, UK

© 2019 by Taylor & Francis Group, LLC
Routledge/Productivity Press is an imprint of Taylor & Francis Group, an Informa business

No claim to original U.S. Government works

Printed on acid-free paper

International Standard Book Number-13: 978-0-367-14552-1 (Hardback)
International Standard Book Number-13: 978-0-367-14550-7 (Paperback)
International Standard Book Number-13: 978-0-429-03228-8 (eBook)

This book contains information obtained from authentic and highly regarded sources. Reasonable efforts have been made to publish reliable data and information, but the author and publisher cannot assume responsibility for the validity of all materials or the consequences of their use. The authors and publishers have attempted to trace the copyright holders of all material reproduced in this publication and apologize to copyright holders if permission to publish in this form has not been obtained. If any copyright material has not been acknowledged please write and let us know so we may rectify in any future reprint.

Except as permitted under U.S. Copyright Law, no part of this book may be reprinted, reproduced, transmitted, or utilized in any form by any electronic, mechanical, or other means, now known or hereafter invented, including photocopying, microfilming, and recording, or in any information storage or retrieval system, without written permission from the publishers.

For permission to photocopy or use material electronically from this work, please access www.copyright.com (http://www.copyright.com/) or contact the Copyright Clearance Center, Inc. (CCC), 222 Rosewood Drive, Danvers, MA 01923, 978-750-8400. CCC is a not-for-profit organization that provides licenses and registration for a variety of users. For organizations that have been granted a photocopy license by the CCC, a separate system of payment has been arranged.

Trademark Notice: Product or corporate names may be trademarks or registered trademarks, and are used only for identification and explanation without intent to infringe.

Visit the Taylor & Francis Web site at
http://www.taylorandfrancis.com

Lean Implementation in Hospital Departments

How to Move from Good to Great Services

Contents

Chapter 1

Introduction

Efficiency and Effectiveness Issues

Efficiency and *effectiveness* are two key words in organizational activities. An organization is said to be efficient if it is able to use all of its resources to produce something valuable without leaving undesirable things. Meanwhile, an organization is said to be effective if it is able to perform in line with what is expected of the organization. These criteria should also be applied to hospitals as organizations in the health system.

A number of efficiency and effectiveness issues can be found at the hospitals in Indonesia. Antibiotics are still inefficiently given to 44%–97% of hospital patients regardless of their need or the appropriateness.[1] In addition, current hospital utilization has tended to decline since 1997.[2] This is due to developments in information technology that encourage people to rely more on self-medication, with various types of drugs available from drug stores or pharmacies. Communities view going to the hospital as more complicated because they must register, wait in line, and pay the consultation fee. Meanwhile, self-medication is seen to be as effective as hospital services in terms of the achievement of the goal to obtain a patient's health, at least for ailments. This is shown in Figure 1.1.

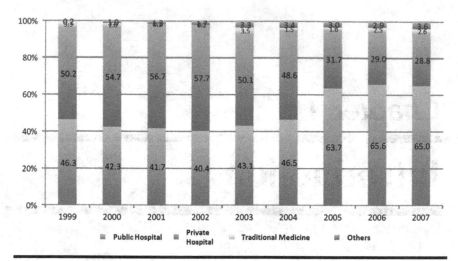

Figure 1.1 Community options for treatment facilities. (From *Indonesia's Doctors, Midwives and Nurses: Current Stock, Increasing Needs, Future Challenges and Options.* **Washington, DC: World Bank, 2009, p. 22.)**

The increasing number of people who seek treatment at health care facilities provides a surge in demand that is too large for public hospitals. Meanwhile, in terms of human resources, decentralization leads to the duplication of tasks and functions, causing inefficiencies of duty implementation.[2] On the other hand, the hospital accreditation system has at least three problems: (1) conflict between the government's role as regulator and assessor, (2) greater focus on input indicators, and (3) lack of integral development.[3]

The Model of Lean Healthcare

Lean is an efficiency improvement model for organizations that is widely used by hospitals today. Lean principles have been gaining great attention since 1990,[4] when Womack, Jones, and Roos published the book *The Machine That Changed the World*, which later became a best Lean seller.[5] The term *Lean* itself was popularized in 1996.[6] Four years later, Lean started to be implemented in service areas around the world. Lean was introduced into healthcare service in the early 2000s.[7] Throughout the decade, Lean was researched and tested together with other models. In the end, Lean tended to show more ability when applied in the *healthcare industry*.[5] In line with these trends, Lean has also reached the strategic realm; it is no longer just in the operational realm.[5] The appointment of Lean in the strategic realm was motivated by research results that found a relationship between Lean implementation and strategic aspects. Strategic aspects include operational management, employee health and quality of life,[4] competitive advantage,[5] and organizational learning.[8] Since then, Lean has attracted various industries throughout the world and is being applied in many operational aspects besides manufacturing.[9]

From here on, we discuss the model of Lean healthcare. Lean healthcare is defined as the "elimination of waste in every field of activity with the aim to reduce inventory, cycle of service time, and cost. So in the end high-quality patient care can be provided in a way that is as efficient, as effective, and as responsive as possible, while retaining economical eligibility of organizations."[10] The model of Lean hospitals, then, briefly interpreted, is hospitals that implement Lean.

The Benefits of Lean Hospitals

The new Lean principles were thoroughly applied in three pioneer hospitals in 2005: Virginia Mason in Seattle, Washington, Flinders in Adelaide, Australia, and ThedaCare in Appleton, Wisconsin.[11] Lean projects successfully showed progress in the hospitals. After that, Lean implementation penetrated various hospitals around the world, and study results show that positive cases related to Lean implementation in hospitals are increasing.

Although Lean focuses on cost reduction and process flow, this focus is the same with sustainable development.[12] Lean and sustainable development have a point of agreement. The meeting point is located at the operational focus in the form of waste reduction.[12] Both sustainable development and Lean equally attempt to reduce waste as much as possible, which means increasing efficiency.

Some empirical evidence has shown the benefits of Lean for hospitals. Vliet et al. in 2010 conducted a study in the cataract clinic at the Rotterdam Eye Hospital in the Netherlands.[13] They found that Lean lowered repeat outpatient procedures by 23% and increased patient access by 42%. Similarly, a study by McCullock et al. in 2010 found that the number of *referred patients* decreased 7%, from 27% to 20%. It is also found that the number of patients increased from 969 to 1114 at a university hospital in the United Kingdom.[14]

In terms of cost savings, a number of studies by Womack et al. at the Virginia Mason Medical Center, report savings of $1 million on hyperbaric examination.[15] In addition, there has been a $1–$3 million savings on endoscopy and $6 million on surgery. A $7.5 million savings in insurance costs was found in studies at Park Nicollet Health Services, Minneapolis, Minnesota.[16] A similar study in LeBonheur Children's Medical Center, Memphis, found a $243,828 savings in supplies.[17]

Empirical evidence regarding the relationship of Lean thinking with service time savings was reported by Taninecz in 2004.[18] Taninecz reports that the response time and emergency services time are accelerating at Hotel-Dieu Grace Hospital, Windsor, Ontario, Canada. Studies of Melanson et al. in 2009 at Brigham and Women's Hospital, Boston, Massachusetts, found that after Lean implementation, the waiting time for laboratory examination decreased from 21 ± 3 minutes to 11 ± 5 minutes.[19]

The efficiency aspect in terms of the work area can also be improved using Lean practices. The studies of Womack et al. in 2005 report that Lean implementation at the Virginia Mason Medical Center reduced the work area 35%–50%.[15]

Actually, there are many other philosophies that can be applied aside from Lean—from the most conventional, standardized systems to the theories of advanced management. From the various formal approaches, there is not one that is superior to the others in all contexts. Each has its own strengths and weaknesses.[20] Indeed, the batch-and-queue system has weaknesses,[21] but it is likely to be easier to apply. Meanwhile, the Uddevalla method, despite encouraging team and individual learning, limits organizational learning and system improvement on the whole.[8,22]

A standardization system, while not sensitive to context, needs to be the basis of quality. In the meantime, a continuous quality improvement system demands a capable human resources infrastructure, but it can have a major impact on product quality.[23]

In the context of healthcare, the management system is important for providing high-quality patient care.[24] In this context, Young and McClean show evidence of the value and measure of Lean implementation in healthcare. They say that there are many reasons that Lean becomes an important element in health service.[7]

Lean has started to be adopted in health services.[7,25] The reason is because Lean thinking promises that the use of resources will be as efficient as possible. Resources in the field of healthcare are very precious and need to be optimized to provide maximum service.[26] Maximum service is seen in terms of both the number of communities served and the quality of services provided. In addition, Lean provides practical benefits in the form of service value flow change, affectionate services, and visible sustainable benefits to the communities, and improves the work system.[10]

The above views show the positive influence of Lean implementation on hospital efficiency. In short, Lean and an emphasis on efficiency are important in the management of health services in the world, including Indonesia. This book tries to provide guidance on and examples of how Lean principles can be implemented in hospitals in Indonesia.

References

1. Hadi, U., Duerink, D.O., Lestari, E.S., Nagelkerke, N.J., Keuter, M., Veld, D.H.I., Suwandojo, E., Rahardjo, E., van den Broek, P., Gyssens, I.C. 2008. Audit of Antibiotic Prescribing in Two Governmental Teaching Hospital in Indonesia. *Clinical Microbiology and Infection*, 14: 698–707.
2. World Bank. 2009. *Indonesia's Doctors, Midwives and Nurses: Current Stock, Increasing Needs, Future Challenges and Options.* Washington, DC: World Bank, p. 22.
3. Irfianti, I. 2011. *Evaluation of Hospital Accreditation in Indonesia by the Hospital Accreditation Commission (Kars): Perception of Hospitals and Isqua Standard.* Master's thesis, University of Gadjah Mada.
4. Landbergis, P.A., Cahill, J., Schnall, P. 1999. The Impact of Lean Production and Related New Systems of Work Organisation on Worker Health. *Journal of Occupational Health Psychology*, 4(2): 108–130. See also: Naylor, B.J., Naim, M.M., & Berry, D. 1999. Leagility: Integrating the Lean and Agile Manufacturing Paradigms in the Total Supply Chain— Strategies for Enriching. *International Journal of Production Economics*, 62(1–2): 107–118; Waring, J.J., Bishop, S. 2010. Lean Healthcare: Rhetoric, Ritual and Resistance. *Social Science & Medicine*, 71: 1332–1340.
5. Wang, Y., Huzzard, T. 2011. The Impact of Lean Thinking on Organizational Learning. OKLC *2011–Making Waves, Knowledge and Capabilities Conference Proceedings*, 1–19. Retrieved from http://www.warwick.ac.uk/fac/soc/wbs/conf/olk c/archive/olkc6/papers/id_128.pdf.
6. Viorel, B., Mihaela, C.A. 2009. Lean Hospital—Conceptualization and Instrumentation. *Ştiinţe Economice Tom*, XVIII: 76.
7. Young, T., McClean, S. 2008. A Critical Look at Lean Thinking in Healthcare. *Quality and Safety in Health Care*, 17(5): 382–386.
8. Adler, P.S., Cole, R.E. 1993. Designed to Learn: A Tale of Two Auto Plants. *Sloan Management Review*, Spring: 33–45.
9. Edwards, T. 2004. The Transfer of Employment Practices across Borders in Multinational Companies. In *International Human Resource Management*, eds. A.-W. Harzing, J.V. Ruysseveldt. London: SAGE, pp. 389–410.

10. Doss, R., Orr, C. 2007. Lean Leadership in Healthcare. *Management*, 17: 11.
11. Fillingham, D. 2007. Can Lean Save Lives? *Leadership in Health Services*, 20(4): 231–241.
12. Dues, C.M., Tan, K.H., Lim, M. 2011. Green as the New Lean: How to Use Lean Practices as a Catalyst to Greening Your Supply Chain. *Journal of Cleaner Production*, 40: 93–100.
13. Vliet, J.E., Sermeus, W., Gaalen, M.C., Vissers, M.J. 2010. Efficacy and Efficiency of Lean Cataract Pathway: A Comparative Study. *Quality and Safety in Healthcare*, 19(6): 13.
14. McCullock, P., Kreckler, S., New, S., Sheena, T., Handa, A., Catchpole, K. 2010. Effect of "Lean" Intervention to Improve Safety Processes and Outcome on a Surgical Emergency Unit. *British Medical Journal (Online)*. Retrieved from https://doi. org/10.1136/bmj.c5469.
15. Womack, J.P., Arthur, P.B., Orest, J.F., Kaplan, G.S., Tousaint, J. 2005. *Going Lean in Health Care*. Institute for Healthcare Improvement. 1–20. Retrieved from https://doi.org/10.1016/j.heal thpol.2015.02.002.
16. Miller, H. 2008. *Lean Healthcare*. Zeeland, MI: Herman Miller.
17. Berczuk, C. 2008. The Lean Hospital. *The Hospitalist*. Retrieved from https://www.the-hospitalist.org/hospitalist/article/123698/l ean-hospital.
18. Taninecz, G. 2007. "Pulling" Lean through a Hospital: Departments at Windsor's Hôtel-Dieu Grace. Lean Enterprise Institute. Retrieved from https://www.lean.org/Search/Do cuments/177.pdf.
19. Melanson, S.E., Goonan, E.M., Lobo, M.M., Baum, J.M., Paredes, J.D., Santos, K.S., Tanasijevic, M.J. 2009. Applying Lean/ Toyota Production System Principles to Improve Phlebotomy Patient Satisfaction and Workflow. *American Journal Clinical Pathology*, 132: 914–919.
20. White, K.R., Griffith, J.R. 2010. *The Well Managed Healthcare Organization*. 7th Edition. Chicago: Aupha, p. 473.
21. Emiliani, M.L. 2004. Improving Business School Courses by Applying Lean Principles and Practices. *Quality Assurance in Education*, 12(4): 175–187; Emiliani, M.L., Stec, D.J. 2004. Using Value-Stream Maps to Improve Leadership. *The Leadership and Organization Development Journal*, 25(8): 622–645; Goland, A., Hall, J., Devereaux, C. 1998. First National Toyota, *The*

McKinsey Quarterly, 4: 59–66; Brady, D. 2000. Why Service Stinks. *BusinessWeek*, 23 October, pp. 118–128; Barron, K. 2000. Hurry Up and Wait. *Forbes*, 16 October, pp. 158–164.

22. MacDuffie, J.P. 1995. Human Resource Bundles and Manufacturing Performance: Organizational Logic and Flexible Production Systems in the World Auto Industry. *Industrial and Labor Relations Review*, 48(2): 197–221.

23. Shortell, S.M., Bennett, C.L., Byck, G.R. 1998. Assessing the Impact of Continuous Quality Improvement on Clinical Practice: What It Will Take to Accelerate Progress. *The Milbank Quarterly*, 76(4): 593–624.

24. West, E. 2001. Management Matters: The Link between Hospital Organisation and Quality of Patient Care. *Quality in Health Care*, 10: 40–48.

25. Dukovska-Popovska, I., Hove-Madsen, V., Nielsen, K.B. 2008. Teaching Lean Thinking through Game: Some Challenges. In *Proceedings of 36th European Society for Engineering Education (SEFI) on Quality Assessment.*

26. Grunden, N., Hagood, C. 2012. *Lean-Led Hospital Design: Creating the Efficient Hospital of the Future.* Boca Raton, FL: CRC Press.

Chapter 2

Lean Principles

Lean Philosophy

Lean is defined as "a long-term growth philosophy through efforts to increase value of customers, society, and economy with the aim to reduce cost, accelerate time to provide intervention, and improve quality through the waste elimination in total."[1] As a philosophy, not all people embrace Lean principles. However, it can also be understood that Lean will depend on human resources. This is because the philosophy lies in the human mind. Various actions do not necessarily make Lean central. For example, human behavior in social relations has nothing to do with Lean.[2] Therefore, the intervention of human resources should be utilized if a company wants to adopt Lean practices. Similarly, a Lean practice does not necessarily provide long-term performance if it is not based on a philosophy inherent in the values that shape attitudes.

Lean practices rely on operating with optimum performance, being responsible for quality, being oriented on the effort to solve the problem, working in small teams, and continually trying to improve oneself.[2] The Lean philosophy originated in Japanese culture, which generally makes the adherents of this philosophy have the aforementioned performance characteristics. Toyota is the most often cited example, and Nike is another. Organizations whose members hold the Lean philosophy tend to save up to 25% compared with companies that do not follow this philosophy.[3]

Lean healthcare is "waste elimination in every service area with the goal of reducing inventory, cycle time of service, and cost. So that high-quality patient care can be provided in a way that is as efficient, as effective, and as responsive as possible, while retaining economical eligibility of organizations."[4] In the context of healthcare, the Lean philosophy demands that a person—not just doctors, but all people—understand the process that happens, observe it, and gather information about it to identify the root of the inefficiency or dissatisfaction of the patient.[5] With this thought, the Lean becomes operational. Not only in the administrative context, but also in a strict standard operating procedure (SOP) such as surgery, Lean is more capable of efficiency, and it is advised not to mix it with other approaches.[6] Once again, Lean is a philosophical system that cannot compromise the ambiguity in human thought.

The emphasis on the humanistic aspect of the Lean philosophy turns the anthropocentrism behavior pyramid of the Industrial Revolution upside down.[4] In the Industrial Revolution era, the pyramid culminated at the director, continued down to the manager, supervisor, and last, the front officer. In the Lean philosophy, because the number of front officers is larger than the number of directors, the apex of the pyramid is occupied by front officers. The role of the board of directors also changes. In the philosophy of the Industrial Revolution, the board of directors gives orders to the front officers; in the Lean philosophy, directors provide support to the front officers. Change from the Industrial Revolution scheme to a Lean one has been seen to bring high quality, low cost, and efficiency into the design and manufacture of products by removing all the waste, which is actually more known by the front officers than the director.[7]

The Lean philosophy framework is described in Table 2.1. It can be seen that the more level decline there is, the higher the variation becomes. Two people from different cultures can create a different ontology from the same assumptions, as well as on the philosophical level or below the philosophical level. On the operational level, Lean becomes so varied that it is difficult to discern whether principles indeed depart from actual Lean or are a modification resulting from the different cultures. Some argue that the original Lean principle is actually only the third principle, waste elimination, while the other principles are adopted from a strategy oriented toward quality rather than efficiency. For example, it can be articulated whether an integrated quality assurance principle of Total Quality Management (TQM) is not Lean. Even so, this principle contains *kaizen*, a *kyosei* component, which means an original component of Lean. Kaizen means "continuous improvement achieved through hands-on experience with a technology."[8]

Table 2.1 Lean Philosophy Framework

Level	Sublevel	Principles
Philosophical Level	Ontology	Humans do not own the universe Humans continue to owe nature Human always multiply while nature is getting smaller
	Epistemology	Efficiency (life must be efficient)
	Axiology	*Kyosei* Continual improvement Award for humanity
Strategic Level	Methodology	Pull system Small lot production Waste elimination (*muda*, Lean thinking) Integrated quality assurance Target costing

Lean Methodology

The core of the strategic level of Lean is waste elimination. Furfari defines Lean thinking as "a methodology to produce high quality products in the shortest amount of time, with the lowest cost as possible by eliminating waste."[9] From this definition, it is understood that Lean thinking is only one of five Lean methodologies. It does not mean that the other four strategic levels are not important, but that they can stand alone without calling themselves Lean. Waste elimination itself is the characteristic of Lean that distinguishes it from other efficiency methods.

Waste is "an activity or behavior that adds to the cost but do not add value as perceived by the final customer."[10] The definition of *Lean thinking* refers to seven types of waste. For some researchers,[11] this concept has been developed into nine wastes (including the seven previous wastes): (1) overproduction, (2) waiting, (3) transportation, (4) overprocessing, (5) inventory, (6) unnecessary motion, (7) defects, (8) employee resistance, and (9) underutilizing people, which is not getting maximum use from them. It can be seen that the last two wastes are more related to human resources rather than physical ones. Employee resistance is "passive resistance, political posturing, or stalling taken by employees in the hope that 'this project will also soon pass.'"[11] Meanwhile, underutilizing people, or not getting maximum use from them, refers to "not involving all employees and not using everyone to their full potential."[11]

If we refer back to the Lean philosophy, the human aspect should be considered. Even so, does the step of judging employee resistance as a form of waste meet the respect principle on humanity? Of course, if the employee has the same philosophy as the company, then there should be no barriers and no need for wasted energy. The emergence of the two last wastes is because the Lean philosophy does not shape employee attitudes but only their behavior. As a result of their duty, employees will demand the right to behave in a Lean manner and refuse to work if they feel they are being treated unfairly. If the company does not instill the Lean philosophy and only directly uses Lean thinking, then the waste that must be omitted becomes more diverse, covering the nine wastes. If the company instills the Lean philosophy and it is accepted by all employees, then the waste that must be removed covers only seven wastes.

Waste elimination then is implemented in the eight operational principles. These principles include (1) layout based on the flow principle, (2) multimachine handling, (3) multiprocess handling, (4) operator loops, (5) U-shaped layout, (6) motion improvement, (7) stopping the line, and (8) autonomation.[12] The flow principle is like running water; ideally, the incoming water should be the same as the outgoing water. Similarly, energy or goods that enter must be equal to those going out so that no waste is left. Multimachine handling means that there are many machines working at once and someone can operate many machines. The same thing applies to multiprocess. The workers who are able to operate many machines and many processes will reduce the amount of workforce required and therefore eliminate the waste.[13]

Operator loops means utilizing workforce to take turns operating the machine. The U shape is more efficient than the S shape (ascending and descending spiral) or I shape as a worker or machine can be placed at the crooked point, and move left and right to do two things at once with minimum energy, rather than have to do one job (I shape) or some work with great energy (S shape). This design has implications for improving motion so as not to tire one out quickly. Stopping the line is done when quality problems occur, so workers can focus on improvements to eliminate waste. If any quality problems can be solved at the root and immediately eliminated, the time will be faster and productivity higher.[14] Automation refers to workers who immediately cluster and cooperate to solve the problem when the line is stopped so that no workers are unproductive during the stoppage.[15]

The principles above are just one variation of many in Lean methodologies. There are at least 26 Lean methodologies that have been collected by researchers.[16] Since there are so many methods of Lean implementation, we will look directly at practical examples to see how these practices are carried out in hospital work units around the world and implemented locally.

References

1. Boos, H., Frank, Z. 2013. Lean Principles in Healthcare Rehabilitation: Suggestions for Implementation. In *Proceedings of the Seventh International Conference on Healthcare Systems & Global Business Issues*. Jaipur: Jaipur National University, p. 170.
2. Birdi, K., Clegg, C., Patterson, M., Robinson, A., Stride, C.B., Wall, T.D., Wood, S.J. 2008. The Impact of Human Resource and Operational Management Practices on Company Productivity: A Longitudinal Study. *Personnel Psychology*, 61: 467–501.
3. Zadek, S. 2004. The Path to Corporate Responsibility. *Harvard Business Review*, 82(12): 125–132, 166.
4. Doss, R., Orr, C. 2007. *Lean Leadership in Healthcare*, White Paper, p. 2. Retrieved from: https://linkinghub.elsevier.com/retrieve/pii/S1472029912002627.
5. Spoerl, B. 2012. How to Get Hospitals to Think 'Lean': 5 Key Principles. *Becker's Hospital Review*. Retrieved from https://www.beckershospitalreview.com/strategic-planning/how-to-get-hospitals-to-think-lean-5-key-principles.html.
6. Inderscience. 2011. Taking the Toyota Approach to Brain Surgery. *ScienceDaily*. Retrieved from https://www.alphagalilco.org/en-gb/Item-Display/ItemId/83013?returnurl=https://www.alphagalileo.org/en-gb/Item-Display/ItemId/83013.
7. Chen, H., Taylor, R. 2009. Exploring the Impact of Lean Management on Innovation Capability. In *PICMET 2009 Proceedings*, Portland, OR, August 2–6, p. 826.
8. Zehner, O. 2012. *Green Illusions: The Dirty Secrets of Clean Energy and the Future of Environmentalism*. Lincoln: University of Nebraska Press, pp. 14–15.

9. Furfari, K. 2009. *The Lean Hospital: What Does It Mean?* University of Colorado Hospital, p. 16. Retrieved from www. uch.edu.
10. Emiliani, M.L. 2006. Improving Business School Courses by Applying Lean Principles and Practices. *Quality Assurance in Education*, 12(4): 175–187.
11. Scott, J.T. 2008. *Managing the New Frontiers: An Introduction to the Fundamentals.* Panama City, FL: Management Education Services, p. 124.
12. Cochran, D.S., Eversheim, W., Kubin, G., Sesterhenn, M.L. 2000. The Application of Axiomatic Design and Lean Management Principles in the Scope of Production System Segmentation. *International Journal of Production Research*, 38(6): 1377–1396.
13. Dohse, K., Ulrich, J., Thomas, N. 1985. From "Fordism" to "Toyotism"? The Social Organization of the Labor Process in the Japanese Automobile Industry. *Politics Society*, 14: 115–146.
14. MacDuffie, J.P. 1995. Human Resource Bundles and Manufacturing Performance: Organizational Logic and Flexible Production Systems in the World Auto Industry. *Industrial and Labor Relations Review*, 48(2): 197–221.
15. Huoy, T. 2005. ICT and Lean Management: Will They Ever Get Along? *Communications & Strategies*, 59: 53–75.
16. Poksinska, B. 2010. The Current State of Lean Implementation in Health Care: Literature Review. *Quality Management in Health Care*, 19(4): 319–329.

Chapter 3

Lean Implementation in the Emergency Unit

Emergency Unit Issues

The emergency unit is a key unit for various intervention programs because it is an entry point for both patients and their families. Intervention here is not merely physical but also psychological, particularly for patients who have emergencies that are not due to disease. Patients who require emergency care not caused by disease (e.g., accidents or violence) are the most in need of psychological intervention because while in the emergency room they experience a "moment of taking wisdom" that has the potential to radically change their lifestyle.[1] The issue, however, is that psychological intervention is rarely given to patients who arrive to the emergency unit for reasons other than disease.

Another issue is that the waiting time of patients in the emergency unit is often high. When patients go to the emergency waiting room, their severity is often assessed. In Canada, patients admitted to the emergency room are assessed based on the Canadian Triage and Acuity Scale (CTAS). In the CTAS, there are five levels of severity. Table 3.1 shows the tolerance of the waiting time for each severity level. Failure to do this assessment could potentially threaten the patient's life.

Table 3.1 Patient Urgency Scale for the Emergency Unit

Level	Name	Example	Intervention
Level 1	Resuscitation	Heart attack	Instant response
Level 2	Emergent	Chest pain	Longest is 15 minutes
Level 3	Urgent	Moderate asthma	Longest is 30 minutes
Level 4	Less urgent	Minor trauma, urinary symptoms	Longest is 60 minutes
Level 5	Nonurgent	Regular cough, sore throat	Longest is 120 minutes

Source: Department of Health and Community Services. 2012. *A Strategy to Reduce Emergency Unit Wait Times in Newfoundland and Labrador.* Newfoundland/Labrador, Canada: p. 12.

The performance of an emergency unit is based on the waiting time, which can be measured by four indicators.[2] The first of these is based on the door to doc (DTD), which is a waiting time from when the patient arrives to the emergency unit to when he or she receives care from a doctor. This indicator shows not only the hospital's commitment to patient safety but also the level of patient satisfaction with the emergency unit service. The second indicator is the length of stay. The length of stay is measured from the patient's arrival until to discharge to home or to another part of the hospital. This indicator shows how well the emergency unit works and gives positive results. A third indicator is *left without being seen.* This refers to the time at which the patient first arrives until he or she leaves without completing the treatment process. Patients can go because they are dissatisfied or because it turns out that they do not require emergency care. The last indicator is patient satisfaction. This indicator clearly shows whether the emergency unit service is satisfactory for patients as a whole.

Often the reason for high waiting times in the emergency unit is a lack of beds in inpatient rooms.[2] This is the output issue emergency units. It means that the hospital must add new and more bedrooms to the existing resources. Within the limitations of the resources, the best way to reduce waiting time is by using the existing resources efficiently.[2]

The second cause of long waiting times in the emergency unit is several nonurgent patients trying to use the emergency unit. This is an input issue to the emergency unit. Moreover, the volume or entry trend of patients to the emergency unit cannot be predicted because it does not depend on a certain season or time.[3] Nonurgent patients may deprive level 1–4 patients from entering. This is especially true in cases when a natural disaster happens, and Indonesia is in the fifth largest country in the world most frequently hit by natural disasters.[4] Under natural disaster conditions, many victims enter the emergency unit. Even so, often the earliest entry of victims is at level 4. This is because these victims are more easily evacuated from the disaster site than the more serious victims (e.g., buried under a building). As a result, when level 1–3 victims arrive, the emergency unit is full, as well as the inpatient rooms.[5] In this case, efficiency measures should be carried out by improving the quality of the CTAS assessment and quality of healthcare for both administrators and staff.[6]

The third issue of the emergency unit service is the knowledge related to diagnoses in the patient's past. The patient or the patient's family who arrive to the emergency unit may be unable to communicate any past diagnoses because of either sudden traumatic events or panic. If a data bank does not exist, then the health service can experience difficulties looking at the outpatient and inpatient experience to guide treatment decisions.[7] In this case, the direct relationship is with the medical record unit and efficiency should be directed at that unit.

The fourth issue is the presence of nonpatients in the emergency unit, especially in the case of a disaster or major disaster. These nonpatient parties are generally the media. The emergency unit is the main unit in the hospital that attracts media attention for various reasons, such as saving lives; overcrowded conditions; the emotional state of patients and their families; the varied case mix ranging from small, innocent children to criminals; the high risk of treatment failure; an overwhelming workload; the amount of distraction; the high-tension atmosphere; and the high risk of complaints, violence, and lawsuits.[8]

The four issues above, in addition to showing the importance of efficiency, also show how the emergency unit depends on good relations with other units in the hospital, such as medical records and inpatient and outpatient units, as well as good relations with the media. The medical records unit provides data access, the inpatient unit provides access to discharged patients, and the outpatient unit gives access to specialists. Still not taken into account are the pharmaceutical unit and the maintenance of facilities.[3] Similarly, the relationship with external parties, especially the media, should be fostered because often healthcare in the emergency unit becomes public relations for the hospital. In addition to the ability of healthcare to face the media, in general hospitals should also build relations with the media so that no news gives a disadvantage to the hospital related to events that occur in the emergency room. Next, we discuss efficiency aspects. Improvement in the efficiency aspects is related either directly or indirectly to good relations aspects, with both other units in the hospital and the media. To summarize, there are four major issues in the emergency unit: completeness of the intervention, waiting time, knowledge management, and public relations issues.

Lean Implementation in the Emergency Unit

Before implementing Lean in the emergency unit, a number of preliminary steps must be taken. There are three factors in successful Lean implementation in emergency units, and these should be prepared in advance. The success factors are (1) employee involvement, (2) management support, and (3) preparedness for change. Holden suggests the following preparations:

1. Prepare for change
2. Take a human-centered approach
3. Secure expertise
4. Get the support of top management and resource allocation
5. Secure leadership
6. Aim to change the culture
7. Adapt Lean for local context
8. Improve in a self-sustainable manner
9. Learn from previous experience[9]

Lean implementation steps in the emergency unit are as follows:[10]

1. Determine value from the patient standpoint in terms of the specific health service given.

   In this step, the hospital needs to hire people to determine value from the patient's standpoint.[11] Value is any operation or process step that contributes directly to the provision of services wanted by patients.[12] Ask patients what they think is disappointing from the services provided by the emergency unit. The questions should be asked when they are not in the service and are in a stable emotional condition. This step is similar to a customer satisfaction survey, but with a different dimension. In search of value, the assessed dimensions include waste dimensions: products (services of nurses, doctors, administration, drugs, rooms, etc.), waiting time, process, error, motion, overlapping, etc. Data collection methods may include interviews, direct observation, focused discussion, telephone interviews, or survey.

2. Identify all the steps in the value stream for the group of
   patients who have the same needs and clearly mark all
   the steps that do not produce value.

   After identifying what is of value in healthcare service
   in an emergency unit from the patients' perspective, the
   team builds a value stream map. A value stream is all
   the actions required to bring a particular service through
   three critical tasks: problem solving, information management, and physical transformation. Problem solving is
   the design of products and processes, information management is the process from taking orders to scheduling
   shipment, and the physical transformation task is deliver-
   ing services from the raw materials into the consumer's
   hands.[10] A value stream map includes all the steps used
   to manage patients from when they first arrive until they
   are discharged from the emergency unit.[11] Figure 3.1 is
   an example of value stream map conditions before Lean
   implementation in the research of Murrell et al.[12]

   Once the value stream map is obtained, the next step is
   to check which of these steps are not needed in the sense
   that they do not add the value stated by the patient. In the
   example above, when viewed from the process perspective, steps that do not add value are the welcome process,
   medical registration, and registration executed separately.
   Assessment can also be done from the perspective of time,
   motion, overproduction, errors, transportation, or inventory.

3. Make the value creation steps appear in a strict order so
   that patients will flow smoothly in the value stream.

   In this step, problem-solving efforts are made to reduce
   the waste that has been found in the value stream map.
   Humans tend to blame, but in Lean implementation it is
   forbidden to blame anyone for the causes of waste.[13] A
   future value stream map is created and used as a common
   goal. The whole idea is directed at how to eliminate the
   waste, and responsibility for doing so is joint. Figure 3.2 is
   a value stream map created by Murrell et al.[12]

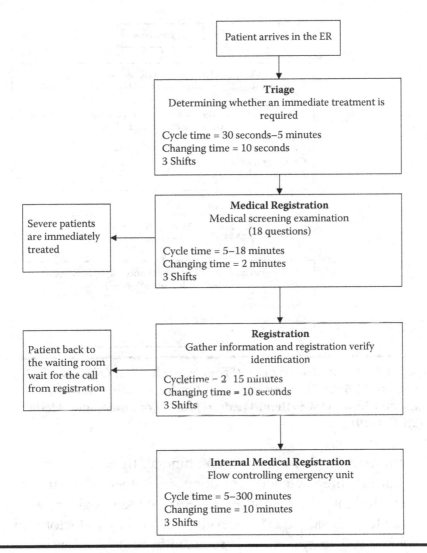

Figure 3.1 Value stream map conditions before Lean implementation. (From Murrell, K.L., Offerman, S.R., Kauffman, M.B. 2011. Applying Lean: Implementation of a Rapid Triage and Treatment System. *Western Journal of Emergency Medicine*, 12(2): 184–191.)

There are three ways to run the plan: (1) total activity, (2) team activity, and (3) individual activity. Total, team, or individual activity is done collectively and distributed immediately after the intervention steps are identified and planned. In the example above, three steps can be

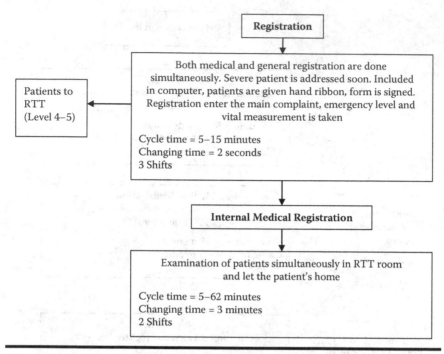

Figure 3.2 Value stream map. (From Murrell, K.L., Offerman, S.R., Kauffman, M.B. 2011. Applying Lean: Implementation of a Rapid Triage and Treatment System. *Western Journal of Emergency Medicine*, 12(2): 184–191.)

put together. Murrell et al. combine all three steps so that the three activities are done simultaneously: data are entered into the computer, a sleeve marker is given, and the form is signed. This step is executed by a doctor and a nurse. The cycle time is reduced from 7–38 minutes to 5–15 minutes. Once this step is done, level 1–3 patients are placed in the examination room and the doctor sees them. Meanwhile, patients classified into level 4 or 5 do not have to wait for a call and go straight into the rapid triage and treatment (RTT) room, which consists of three small examination rooms, a couple of chairs, and some RTT doctors. RTT doctors conduct examinations with the patients in chairs as long as they do not mind. If the patients object and the examination room is in use, then they must wait for a small examination room to become available. RTT nurses and doctors must communicate intensely and complement each other so that issues and questions are answered and resolved.

4. Ensure that all healthcare professionals in the unit cooperate in getting patients through the value stream.

   This step is clear. All parties must cooperate and be committed to directing patients to the new value stream that has been created. Without consistency, the designed value stream can fail.

5. Pursue perfection.

   The pursuit of perfection in terms of Lean is *kaizen*. In general, it is an evaluation form but with continuous follow-up. Assessment of the value stream should be done every week to see if anything needs further improvement or should be viewed from a different perspective than from the previous week.

References

1. Corbin, T.J., Rich, J.A., Bloom, S.L., Delgado, D., Rich, L.J., Wilson, A.S. 2011. Developing a Trauma-Informed, Emergency Department–Based Intervention for Victims of Urban Violence. *Journal of Trauma & Dissociation*, 12(5): 510–525.
2. Department of Health and Community Services. 2012. *A Strategy to Reduce Emergency Unit Wait Times in Newfoundland and Labrador.* Newfoundland/Labrador, Canada, p. 12.
3. Mukhi, N. 2013. Reducing Patient Throughput Time in Emergency Units by Resolving Bottlenecks. In *Proceedings of the 7th International Conference on Healthcare Systems and Global Business Issues*, Jaipur, India, January 3–6, pp. 103–110.
4. Guha-Sapir, D., Hoyois, P., Below, R. 2013. *Annual Disaster Statistical Review 2012: The Numbers and Trends.* Brussels: CRED, p. 1.
5. Auf der Heide, E. 1989. *Disaster Response: Principles of Preparation and Coordination.* St. Louis, MO: Mosby, p. 109.

6. Liao, H.-C., Liaw, S.-J., Hu, P.-M., Lee, K.-T., Chen, C.-M., Wang, F.-L. 2002. Emergency Unit Patients Who Leave without Being Seen by a Doctor: The Experience of a Medical Center in Northern Taiwan. *Chang Gung Medical Journal*, 25(6): 367–373.
7. Silow-Carroll, S., Edwards, J.N., Rodin, D. 2012. Using Electronic Health Records to Improve Quality and Efficiency: The Experiences of Leading Hospitals. *Issue Brief (Commonwealth Fund)*, 17: 1–40.
8. Chung, C., Lai, K.K. 2006. Meeting the Media: Friend or Foe? *Hong Kong Journal of Emergency Medicine*. Retrieved from: https:// journals.sagepub.com/doi/pdf/10.1177/102490790601300205.
9. Holden, R.J. 2010. Lean Thinking in Emergency Units: A Critical Review. *Annals of Emergency Medicine*, 57(3): 265–278.
10. Rosmulder, R.W. 2011. *Improving Healthcare Delivery with Lean Thinking: Action Research in an Emergency Unit*. PhD dissertation, University of Twente, the Netherlands, p. 129.
11. Dickson, E.W., Anguelov, Z., Vetterick, D., Eller, A., Singh, S. 2009. Use of Lean in the Emergency Unit: A Case Series of 4 Hospitals. *Annals of Emergency Medicine*, 54(4): 3.
12. Murrell, K.L., Offerman, S.R., Kauffman, M.B. 2011. Applying Lean: Implementation of a Rapid Triage and Treatment System. *Western Journal of Emergency Medicine*, 12(2): 184–191.
13. Farrell, J.M. 2009. *10 Steps to Lean: A Manual for Implementation of Lean in Hospitals*. Bangkok, Thailand: Janet M. Farrell & Associates, p. 10.

Chapter 4

Lean Implementation in the Outpatient Unit

Outpatient Unit Issues

The outpatient unit is a second gate at the hospital, in addition to the emergency department. The outpatient unit provides services to patients who have complaints that are not urgent and can be addressed without their having to stay in the hospital. This unit provides support not only for the patient but also for people around the patient. This is shown by lifting the burden of a companion physically, psychologically, socially, and economically.[1]

Such benefits have to be balanced with various issues relating to the performance of the outpatient unit. Patient satisfaction with the outpatient unit is affected by the length of the consultation period, the objective average waiting time, appreciation and acknowledgment from health workers for waiting patiently, the waiting time that can be tolerated by patients[2] and interactions between healthcare workers and patients.[3] From those factors, the waiting time always gets the spotlight.[4] The highest waiting time in hospitals generally occurs in the outpatient unit. There are three types of waiting time: preprocess, in process, and postprocess. Preprocess waiting time occurs prior to service delivery. Unfortunately, this type of waiting time is the easiest to rate negatively compared with the other types. In-process waiting occurs while the patient is being examined, for example, waiting for a physician who answered his or her phone during the exam. An example of postprocess waiting time is waiting for a medication to take effect. Generally the most problematic waiting time is the preprocess type.

If indeed the waiting time is unavoidable, there are steps that hospitals can take. The hospital can provide information to the patients regarding the reasons for the wait to prevent patients from becoming unsatisfied.[2] Another step is to thank patients for waiting after the process has finally begun. The waiting environment also affects the perception of the waiting time by patients. A comfortable environment, such as one that has musical accompaniment or a fountain, can change the perception of patients on waiting time. Park Nicollet Health Services in Minneapolis, for example, builds outpatient waiting rooms with exterior and interior designs inspired by rivers and wetlands. They include stones from the local area, the artwork of local artists, recycled granite, and an educational display.[5]

Of course, the best way is to not have a waiting time at all. Waiting time is an urgent issue since over time the use of outpatient facilities in Indonesian hospitals has increased. In 2001, the rate of use of outpatient units in public hospitals in Indonesia was still below 2%, but in 2007 it reached 2%.[6] The same trend occurred in private hospitals, even though the percentage is low. Surkesnas 2004, or Indonesia Health Survey, reveals that 26.1%, or a quarter, of the outpatients feel that the waiting time in hospitals is unsatisfactory.

In addition to waiting time, medication errors and therapy issues are other issues in outpatient units. Not all of these errors are from the healthcare. Patients and their companions are also essential in ensuring safety from the use of medical therapy. Unfortunately, Surkesnas (2004) reveals that the issue of patient and companion involvement in health decisions in outpatient units has the highest dissatisfaction in Indonesian hospitals. About 32.8%, or nearly one-third, of patients feel excluded in outpatient decision making.

Surkesnas (2004) also shows Indonesian patient dissatisfaction on ward services. It covers hospitality (13.6%), information availability (24.1%), personal consultation (27.3%), freedom of choice (26.8%), and cleanliness (18.3%).[6] In general, only 59.7% of the outpatients in Indonesian hospitals are satisfied with the service; the remaining are somewhat satisfied (32.3%), somewhat dissatisfied (7.2%), and dissatisfied (0.9%).[6]

Lean Case Studies in Outpatient Units

Strategies to overcome the above issues can be implemented through Lean. Many Lean implementation studies have been conducted hospital outpatient units and shown positive effects. One covers the case of Brigham and Women's Hospital in Boston where the waiting time was decreased from 21 minutes to 5 minutes, patient satisfaction with the waiting times was improved up to 50%, and consultation time was reduced by 20%.[7] Lean implementation at a National Health Service (NHS) hospital resulting in a 4% reduction in canceled consultations and a 30% reduction of nurse walking distance.[8] Lean implementation at Sentara Norfolk General Hospital, Virginia, was successful in increasing profits from outpatient procedures to $9.1 million, 32% higher than expected.[9]

Learning from the experiences of the hospital on the ward unit, Lean implementation steps can be done in two ways: through one's own version or copied from any existing version. Your own version can be carried out as follows:

1. Ask for a commitment from the staff, leaders, and managers to work together to improve the system. There will be an increase in the workload in the beginning, but in time the workload will likely be less than it would be had Lean not been implemented.

2. Create a joint committee with outpatient staff to set common goals in the Lean process. The committee should
   study all the processes in the outpatient unit and determine what areas need improvement. Knowledge of these
   steps is obtained through preparation and observation of
   information from the value stream map, from the patient's
   arrival to discharge. From this map, things found can
   discarded or condensed. In addition, the value stream
   map is useful for preparing the electronic health record
   (EHR). Figure 4.1 shows the value stream maps of Sentara
   Hospital before and after Lean implementation. In the initial value stream map, the process of login orders reached
   27 steps. The committee deleted a large number of steps,
   and now there are only eight. This map describes the
   value stream across the entire Sentara Hospital unit, but
   you can modify it for only the outpatient unit.
3. Besides observations on the value stream map, the committee will need to observe communication aspects
   between the outpatient unit and other units in the hospital. In this way, information issues can be found and
   improved. After that, the committee should focus on
   determining goals for specific areas. For example, in the
   case of Brigham and Women's Hospital, the committee decided to focus on patient waiting time and overall
   patient satisfaction. The committee may use the framework discussed above for problems in the hospital outpatient unit, in the form of either factors that influence
   patient satisfaction or patient satisfaction indicators of
   Surkesnas 2004. The observations of committees on value
   stream maps show six factors (including the environment) and seven indicators. The committee should review
   these factors and indicators and then decide which ones
   should be prioritized for improvement. Other factors and
   indicators will follow as an interaction will surely happen.
   However, the committee still has to see if there is a negative interaction where focusing on and strengthening one

ORDER ENTRY PROCESS

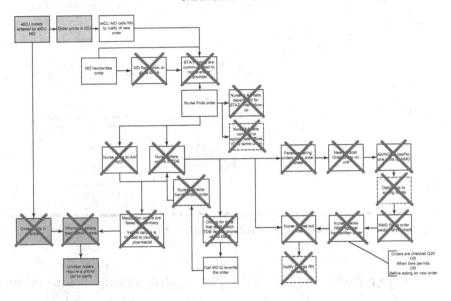

Streamlined:

ORDER ENTRY PROCESS

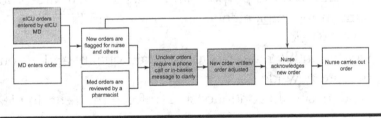

Figure 4.1 Fixed value stream map for Sentara Hospital. (From Silow-Carroll, S., Edwards, J.N., Rodin, D. 2012. Using Electronic Health Records to Improve Quality and Efficiency: The Experiences of Leading Hospitals. *Commonwealth Fund,* **17: 20.)**

area actually has a negative impact on other indicators or factors. Figure 4.2 will help you disassemble the outpatient performance in a hospital.

4. Hold an intensive and structured workshop to find a solution and then conduct a trial of the strategy in real time. The workshop can last 4 days. On the first day, the activities carried out are training related to the Lean principles

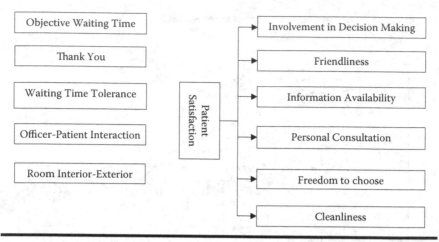

Figure 4.2 Framework of service outpatient unit.

and philosophy. On the second day, the committee pres-
ents a problem and all the participants brainstorm to come
up with a solution. Days 3 and 4 are used to conduct a
trial of solutions and measure whether they are effective.
5. Provide updates every few days to see whether the staff
has achieved the purpose and whether there are problems in the implementation. Updates can be done up to
seven weeks.
6. Hold monthly meetings to maintain quality and accom-
modate new ideas.
7. Leaders should continuously reinforce the Lean implementation by giving daily praise to the staff and offering
specific examples of how Lean is successfully improving
outpatient efficiency.

When using an existing version, you must consider whether
the practical examples presented below are relevant to your
outpatient unit. Actually, these steps are the result of the seven
steps above. Some of the practical steps are as follows:

1. Deli counter-style number system. Patients who wait are
given a number to indicate their position in the queue.
The number for the patients most recently called is clearly

stated on an LCD board. Signs are made to with the times of polyclinic operations and the busiest period. In this way, patients can know when they can get services. They also can choose to go home and come back another time, when the polyclinic is not busy.

2. Early notification from the polyclinic regarding information or requested samples. In the case of Brigham and Women's Hospital, patients are asked to collect urine samples themselves while waiting to save the time of sample collection.

3. Eliminate activities that do not add value. For this, one needs to perform their own step version. In the case of Brigham and Women's Hospital, steps that did not add value were examination of excessive specimen, logging when the sample canister was sent through the pneumatic tube, and answering the phone for common questions.

4. Use an outpatient coordinator to greet and call the patients. Rather than each polyclinic calling patient separately, one coordinator is given the task to welcome arriving patients, hand out queue numbers, and call the patients once it is their turn.

5. Reduce inventory, improve the ability to find lost files, make room to store a patient's medical record 1 day earlier, and redesign the layout of the lounge.

6. EHR (or electronic medical record) design. This step needs value stream mapping (see Figure 4.1). Consult software designers to create software that is specifically designed to handle electronic medical records. The EHR allows hospitals to store and retrieve patient information in detail, for use by all parties, including the patients themselves.

References

1. Reinhard, S.C., Given, B., Pettlick, N.H., Bemis, A. 2008. Supporting Family Caregivers in Providing Care. In *Patient Safety and Quality: An Evidence-Based Handbook for Nurses*, Rockville, MD: Agency for Healthcare Research and Quality: p. 62.

2. De Man, S., Vandaele, D., Gemmel, P. 2004. *The Waiting Experience and Customer Perception of Service Quality in Outpatient Clinics.* Universiteit Gent Working Paper, p. 2.
3. Holden, R.J. 2011. Lean Thinking in Emergency Department: A Critical Review. *Annals of Emergency Medicine,* 57(3): 265–278.
4. Vissers, J. 1979. Selecting a Suitable Appointment System in an Outpatient Setting. *Medical Care,* XVII: 1207–1220.
5. Buggy, J.M., Nelson, J. 2006. Applying Lean Production in Healthcare Facilities. *Implications,* 6(5): 4.
6. Rokx, C., Schieber, G., Harimurti, P., Tandon, A., Somanathan, A. 2009. *Health Financing in Indonesia: A Reform Road Map.* Washington, DC: World Bank, p. 65.
7. Melanson, S.E.F., Goonan, E.M., Lobo, M.M., Baum, J.M., Paredes, J.D., Santos, K.S., Gustafson, M.L., Tanasijevic, M.J. 2009. Applying Lean/Toyota Production System Principles to Improve Phlebotomy Patient Satisfaction and Workflow. *American Journal of Clinical Pathology,* 132: 914–919.
8. Nasiri, S.D. 2009. *Lean Thinking and Queue Modelling in Healthcare.* Lancaster, UK: Lancaster University Management School, p. 14.
9. Silow-Carroll, S., Edwards, J.N., Rodin, D. 2012. Using Electronic Health Records to Improve Quality and Efficiency: The Experiences of Leading Hospitals. *Commonwealth Fund,* 17: 20.

Chapter 5

Lean Implementation in the Ward Unit

The Quality of Care of Services in the Ward Unit

The ward unit is where patients have the longest contact with the hospital. Satisfaction with the quality of the ward unit is the most important indicator for a hospital because it takes into account the hospital services from various aspects. The most important component of ward unit quality is care service quality. This is because during hospitalization, patients form an emotional and interpersonal bond with their nurse.[1]

Assessment of ward unit quality care services contains five indicators: compassion, close relationships, personal care, uncertainty reduction, and reliability.[1] All these indicators show the supportive leadership of nurses.[2] Compassion is the sympathetic awareness of nurses of the susceptibility of each patient and the great desire of the nurses to reduce patient suffering. Nurses build close relationships with patients, such as family relationships and friendships, which involve elements such as trust, pleasure, and affection. Personal care means that nurses are sensitive to the situation and needs of the patients, are flexible and can adapt to these needs, and are able to manage excessive patients to achieve optimal healing. Uncertainty reduction means that nurses provide information on the progress and status of the patients so that the patients are not doubtful of their health conditions in the future. Reliability means that the nurses are able to maintain a commitment to patients, provide quick services, and do maintenance tasks accurately and competently.

Patient satisfaction on ward services does not include just satisfaction with the nurse care. A physician service, for example, is also an indicator of patient satisfaction. A charismatic physician will bring good perception about ward quality, as opposed to physicians who do not have charisma.[2] Physician and nurse services are then determined by their commitment factor to work and their satisfaction with their work.[2] There is a measuring tool called the Patient Judgment System (PJS) that can be used to assess patient satisfaction on ward service.[3] The PJS includes 10 indicators: admission, daily care, information, nurse services, physician services, supporting staff services, lifestyle, release, bills, and total process. In addition to these indicators, the availability of drugs, waiting times, and administrative workload are also often used to determine the perception of ward service quality.[4] The availability of drugs on the ward is an issue that needs attention because in this field, many hospitals still use manual methods to collect and report drug data.[5]

Patient satisfaction with ward services is not the only factor that sets expectations for the intention to reuse ward services in the future. Another important factor is the environmental factor.[1] It includes location proximity and parking. Other environmental factors may be in the form of the transfer speed from the emergency room to the ward.[6]

From the description above, we can see that the decision to choose a hospital for ward services is complex and consists of many factors. A factor map from the explanation above is shown in Figure 5.1. Some of these factors include efficiency, which means that they can be improved if the hospital or ward unit implements Lean. Location factors might be impossible to change because a hospital cannot affect the

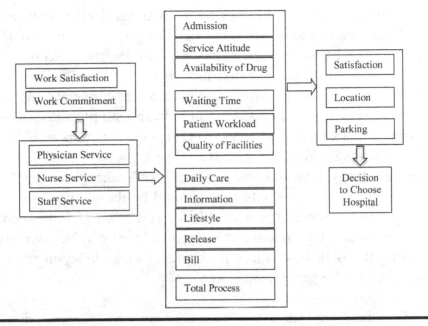

Figure 5.1   Options framework for hospital ward.

environment it is in, who chooses to live there, or how many competitors may be present in the future. Parking and satisfaction factors can be improved by the Lean strategy.

Lean Case Studies in Ward Units

A number of Lean studies are also available for seeing how Lean can be used to improve the quality of ward services. Lean implementation at the Wake Forest Baptist Medical Center (WFBMC), Winston-Salem, North Carolina, which is directed specifically at the pharmacy section of the ward, increased the timely delivery of drugs from 38% to 59% in the first month, 61% in the second month, and 63% in the third month.[7] Lean implementation at the Virginia Mason Medical Center (VMMC) provides a fascinating picture. In the third month after implementation, staff walking distance decreased from 5818 steps to 846 steps, the required time to fulfill one morning work cycle of nurses for all patients decreased from 240 minutes to 126 minutes, the percentage of calls within a period of 4 hours decreased from 5.5% to 0%, the percentage of nurse time for care activities that do not add value decreased from 68% to 10%, and within one care cycle the time to search for and collect materials and supplies decreased from 20 minutes to 3 minutes.[8] Lean implementation at Cincinnati Children's Hospital (CCH) successfully saved 208 length-of-stay days and saved $60,480 for Medicaid patients.[9]

The Lean implementation conducted by the above three hospitals can serve as an example for you to try to implement in your ward unit. Systematic steps by VMMC can be adopted to find the right way to face problems of inefficiency in your ward unit. The general steps are:

1. Make a workshop with a team of eight people, including nurses, technicians, and patients. This team should focus on the workflow of nurses on the ward unit.
2. The team should look for weaknesses in the workflow using a value map.
3. The team will then build a number of indicators as the baseline, which will be corrected in Lean implementation.
4. The team will formulate Lean steps that can be applied to resolve this issue.
5. Implementation is done.

Here are practical steps that can be used if you choose to directly use an example:

1. Lean implementation performed by WFBMC was directed specifically at the ward pharmacy. WFBMC considered the fact that the output of the pharmaceutical products could be in the thousands and the pharmaceutical product fulfillment target could be specific depending on each medication. WFBMC determined that a solution to improve efficiency would be to use PharmTrac.PD. This is a process

management and medication tracking solution based on barcodes and mobile devices that provides guidance on the process and performance of the ward pharmacy. It reduces consequences from late deliveries, missing medication, and requests from staff nurses. This solution approximately equals those in Chapter 4 as it relates to EHR use.

2. The administration of rooms or medication to patients should be made in a U-shaped mobile zone so as to minimize mileage. This is especially necessary if the administration of medication or rooms for the patients is currently done in a long, linear hallway.

3. Sort the morning shift to meet all working aspects with one patient before moving to another patient.

4. Standardize the reporting on all patients so that it can be done by everyone who performs the work. Reporting and documentation are done at the patient's bedside by involving the patient, if possible.

5. Restock the inventory box with supplies only as required by the *kanban* system. Kanban is a management system that guarantees production through communication, which is at the point of use. The point of use is at the patient's bedside, thus cutting the time spent by nurses to find and take supplies to the patient to treat them.

6. Make a standardized record that contains all the patient's needs before leaving the room and moving to other patients. This step anticipates the patient's needs before the needs are present.

7. Store inventory at the point of use, and nurses and technicians report placement at the patient's bedside. This also allows the nurses to increase patient satisfaction by building interpersonal relationships with them. Nurses and technicians also do report and treatment planning together with the patient's involvement.

8. A visual flag system in the inventory box at the point of use demonstrates the need for new provisions in a timely manner.

9. The Lean steps conducted at CCH are unique and don't
   seem to make sense at first. After consulting with a Lean
   expert, CCH lowered the amount of bed use in the ward.
   The main purpose was actually to get as much revenue
   as possible from patients, and therefore only patients who
   have plentiful resources can be received in CCH. The
   baseline showed that rich patients were not getting rooms
   because the ward was filled with poor patients. Similarly,
   certain patients experience financial loss due to the use
   of Medicaid (the equivalent of Assurance) facilities, where
   the financing is based on the bed instead of the disease
   type. This provides an additional cost of $60,480 to be
   borne by CCH.

Refusing patients with cheap payment billing is certainly
not ethical, so this step is not implemented by CCH. CCH
uses evidence-based treatment directed to the local community around the hospital. After a demographic review, it was
found that poor patients live around the hospital. These poor
patients only suffer from diseases such as asthma, bronchitis,
hay fever without a clear source, and gastroenteritis. CCH then
works with the family doctor (in the case of Indonesia, we can
cooperate with health centers) to conduct supervision of the
environment. The family doctor visits the houses and provides
health services; thus, people who would usually go to the doctor and enter the ward no longer have to thanks to the community doctor's regular visit. As a result, in 10 years there has
been a decline in the visit to the CCH ward of patients with
asthma by 376%, bronchitis 436%, fever without clear reason
586%, and gastroenteritis 6%. The result of this decline is the
inclusion of rich patients who really need the ward, making
it possible for the hospital to get a higher profit. Now instead
of the ward at CCH always being full, it is always available for
patients who desperately need it. Communities are also helped
because patients do not need to come to CCH. In this way,
CCH also saves 208 length-of-stay days.

References

1. Koerner, M.M. 2000. The Conceptual Domain of Service Quality for Inpatient Nursing Services. *Journal of Business Research*, 48: 267–283.
2. Ratnamiasih, I., Govindaraju, R., Prihartono, B., Sudirman, I. 2012. Leadership and Hospital Service Quality. In *3rd International Conference on Business and Economic Research Proceeding*, pp. 1468–1476.
3. Aday, L.A., Cornelius, L.J. 2005. *Designing and Conducting Health Surveys: A Comprehensive Guide*. 3rd Edition. Jossey-Bass, p. 286.
4. Fritzen, S. 2005. *From Infrastructure to Institutions: Reforming Primary Health Care in Vietnam*. Singapore: National University of Singapore, p. 21.
5. Agency for Healthcare Research and Quality. 2009. Medication Turnaround Time in the Inpatient Setting. AHRP Publication No. 09-0045. Rockville, MD: Agency for Healthcare Research and Quality.
6. Farrell, J.M., et al. 2009. *10 Steps to Lean: A Manual for Implementation of Lean in Hospitals*, Bangkok, Thailand: Janet M. Farrell & Associates. See also: Manos, A., Sattler, M., Alukal, G. 2006. *Make Healthcare Lean, Quality Process* 39(7): 24–30.
7. Chou, J., Peaty, N., Strickland, J.M. 2013. *Measuring, Evaluating, and Improving Medication Distribution Process and Performance Metrics in an Inpatient Pharmacy: The Value of Medication Tracking, On Time Delivery, and Pharmacy Analytics*. White Paper. Plus Delta Technologies, LLC.
8. Nelson-Peterson, D.L., Leppa, C.J. 2007. Creating an Environment for Caring Using Lean Principles of the Virginia Mason Production System. *The Journal of Nursing Administration*, 37(6): 287–294.
9. Hines, S., Luna, K., Lofthus, J., Stelmokas, D. 2008. Becoming a High Reliability Organization: Operational Advice for Hospital Leaders. AHRQ Publication No. 08-0022. Rockville, MD: Agency for Healthcare Research and Quality, p. 71.

Chapter 6

Lean Implementation in the Central Surgical Unit

Central Surgical Unit Issues

The central surgical unit of a hospital is characterized by similar procedures everywhere. Minor differences include small adjustments and variations due to the surgeons or patients.[1] The unit contains a large amount of specialist equipment that is used for routine procedures by the surgeons. Sudden changes to the procedures, for example, a change in a routine or the ways of working, can make them difficult to perform and cause stress for the workers in this unit. This is because they are accustomed to the strict routine and procedures, and for obvious reasons, an error in the implementation of the procedures may result in death for surgical patients. Yet, change is needed, since both technology and new surgical techniques continue to emerge, replacing the old procedures and because there are problems in efficiency.

The efficiency problems on a unit can be seen from the cases in Indonesia. There, the surgical patients are given excessive antibiotics.[2] About 42% of surgical prophylaxis antibiotics given to the patients is unnecessary. In fact, almost all (90%) surgical patients who stay more than four days in the surgical unit are administered antibiotics, compared with general patients, of whom only 14%–32% get antibiotics. The purpose of the administration of prophylactic antibiotics is to provide a clean surgery, so they are consumed several days before and several days after the surgery. However, often this administration is not based on objective clinical diagnosis criteria or evidence of microbiological infection. This problem is found not only in Indonesia but also in many developed countries. Similar studies in the Netherlands, for example, have found that 46% of antibiotic administration and use in the surgical unit is excessive. The reasons for such high administration are the backgrounds of the different medical personnel and peer pressure.[3] The surgeon is not a specialist who can assess whether a person is in need of antibiotics. Likewise, the developing medical culture encourages physicians to prescribe antibiotics.

The problem is rooted in the tradition of the central surgical unit prioritizing safety. Studies show that nurses in the surgical unit always place a higher value on patient safety than nurses in other units.[4] In the surgical unit, patient safety intervention is easier to oversee and is more visible here than in other units due the more standardized procedures.[5] For example, the safety checklist for the central surgical unit can reach 78 items—more than any other department in the hospital.[6] In addition, the education level of nurses in the surgical unit tends to be higher, so they have a lot of knowledge on patient safety.[7] Patient safety is always prioritized, and it is better to be wasteful than to have the patients not survive. This approach is correct, but it would be more so if the number of antibiotics administered was appropriate and in accordance with the needs. Moreover, excessive antibiotics actually trigger the evolution of bacteria because they combat only weak bacteria, leaving the strong bacteria, which can have a greater effect on patients than had they not been administered antibiotics.

Other characteristics of the unit include the psychology of the patients[8] Surgery is a special experience for patients, and despite potentially promising healing, it also often raises fear. Research shows that patients who are in inpatient rooms for several hours after the surgery have less chances of death than patients who are hospitalized for 7–10 days.[9] How well the psychology of patients is dealt with both before and after surgery can have a positive impact on the welfare of patients. Deaths are actually a form of inefficiency in the form of failed products. Hospitals that do not provide interventions that can psychologically improve the welfare of patients preoperatively and postoperatively can therefore be said to be wasteful.

Lean Case Studies in Central Surgical Units

Although the central surgical unit has complex characteristics, Lean studies have been successfully carried out on this unit. Serrano and Slunecka (2006) have used the value stream map methodology in the surgical unit, which is directed at patient satisfaction, cost savings, and time to set up the room and has given positive results.[10] McCullock et al. (2010) at the John Radcliffe Hospital, Oxford, England, have found that the quality increases from 28% to 149% and referral rates decrease from 27% to 20%. Studies of Brooker in a pediatric surgical unit in 1997 showed success in changing nurses' habits by educating them to make the best decision in fitting bandages for child injuries to reduce errors that could cause serious infection.[11] Likewise, studies of Nies et al. found that the Clinical Decision Support (CDS) tool is capable of reducing waste in blood tests in the cardiovascular surgical unit.[12]

The following steps were adopted from three studies of Lean implementation conducted in the central surgical unit of various hospitals. These steps are divided based on the goals that they are trying to achieve.

1. Goal: Eliminate errors
     Case example: Knee infection
     Case location: Appleton Medical Surgical Care Unit[13]

Lean tool: Standardized work (A3)

Steps:

a. The unit manager and unit start the day by reviewing the statistical sheets to find any risk to quality and safety that may have occurred during the previous shift. In the case of Appleton, the team found a knee infection.

b. Further review of the data is done with a longer time span. In the case of Appleton, the team found that there were four knee infection cases in the last nine months. Therefore, this can be regarded as a case of error, which means that a form of waste should be eliminated.

c. The manager makes a plan to immediately determine whether the unit can prevent the next knee infection. In this plan, the next step is to observe all knee surgeries to determine the cause of complications.

d. The manager asks the volunteers to get together and develop A3 to find the cause of complications. A3 is a Lean tool consisting of three stages: (1) study the problem, (2) propose solutions, and (3) implement the changes. The first stage is done in the form of fishbone analysis and stratification data based on the physician, time, operating room, and so on. Fishbone analysis is a diagram used to find the components of a problem and explore all the potential or tangible causes that result in destruction or failure. In the case of Appleton, the volunteers found that the cause of the problem was the suture.

e. The team then conducts an interview with a doctor about their experience with the issue, and the suspected doctor is monitored. In the Appleton case, a team of physicians interviewed the doctors related to the infection experiences and found that one physician did not have any experience with the infection at all. The team monitored this doctor and founds that they use a different type of suture.

f. The investigation takes time, and during the investigation the supervisory unit must report progress to the manager every day. The manager gives a report to the vice president. At Appleton, the investigation process takes 3 months, and at the end of the investigation the conclusion was that the infection was caused by a type of suture used by two physicians. The next step of the A3 process was to propose a solution, which was to change the sutures used. This solution was implemented by providing training to physicians, and after six months there was no longer grade 1 knee infection cases at Appleton.

2. Goal: Achieve and increase daily improvement
   Case example: Business performance system
   Case location: Appleton Medical Care (AMC) and Theda
   Clark Medical Center (TCMC)[13]
   Lean tool: Continual improvement
   Steps:
   a. Compose a project team. The team is tasked with examining the issues that currently exist in the hospital.
   b. Perform inverted fishbone analysis. The best fishbone diagrams determine what components are needed to achieve the unit's goal. In the case of TCMC, the inverted fishbone consists of five components: the leadership's standardized work, visual control improvement, problem solving and corrective action, leadership discipline, and leadership development.
   c. Establish a focus group. A focus group aims to find problems from the perspective of the manager. In this focus group, the staff is involved. The goal of a focus group discussion is to find the root of the problems faced by a hospital. In the case of TCMC, the root of the problem was the absence of a systematic management approach that enabled the manager to clearly define problems, organize solutions, and achieve clear performance goals.
   d. Update A3. In this step, the findings of the focus group are made input for improvement. In the case of

TCMC, four basic issues were found: (1) the team was not positioned to view, prioritize, and pursue improvement opportunities; (2) the unit leaders had style management variations without a structured management reporting system; (3) the manager struggled to maintain progress using a makeshift manner; and (4) each leader had their own way of leading.

e. Conduct a quick improvement event. This event is intended to build standardized work to solve issues that found in the previous step. In the case of TCMC, the event took place in two weeks. The result was a list of standardized work that must be adhered to by the leadership. The standardized work consists of eight guides: (1) how to prepare a daily statistical sheet; (2) how to manage daily review; (3) how to prepare work schedules; (4) how to teach, train, and supervise; (5) how to collect data for monthly performance meetings; (6) what to report on at the monthly performance meetings; (7) how to create and run solutions and communicate them; and (8) how to share, report, and raise problems or information at the higher organizational level.

f. Establish a steering committee (SC). The project team is replaced by an SC that consists of all project team members plus new members from nonmedical fields to provide a new perspective for the team. SC members are selected based on certain criteria. The SC team is tasked to develop jobs and move the work in the implementation stage. In the case of TCMC, the criteria used were as follows: (1) must be able to speak well with each other about the outcome, either good or bad; (2) must be able to trust each other so that they can criticize each other; and (3) must agree that there is no limit in the act.

g. Implementation. Examples of cases of knee infection in the first case example are one of the implementations of standard work that has been developed in stages a to f above. Still many other cases are reported in the consolidated results of TCMC's research. Within 15 weeks of implementation, the results obtained included an increase in productivity by 1%–11% in all units in two hospitals. For the surgical unit, a 4% increase in productivity for TCMC and an 11% increase in productivity for AMC were found. In addition, failed cases decreased to 35% in TCMC's surgical unit; 9% efficiency of beds in wards and cancellation of inpatients were reduced by 70%.

3. Goal: Improve patient satisfaction
   Case example: Resource utilization
      Case location: Ronald Reagan UCLA Medical Center
                     Department of Neurosurgery[14]
   Lean tool: Standardized work
   Steps:
   a. Create an SC team.
   b. Create patient flow to find waste in a process. This is done with value stream mapping (see Chapter 2).
   c. Create operator flow to find steps in every activity in order to develop standardized work.
   d. Interview the patient care coordinator (PCC) to determine the value of each step of the operator, the issues faced, and any deficiencies. In the case of UCLA, the problem faced was that the process of authorizing insurance did not add value but added wait time for the patient and a volume of phone calls that was beyond the PCC's ability to handle, and there was no mechanism to confirm the patient appointment.
   e. Build consensus through SC and staff meetings.
   f. Find opportunities for improvement in the value stream. In the case of UCLA, the intake of new patients was centralized, insurance authorization was centralized, and appointment reminders were automated.
   g. Implementation. All opportunities are implemented. A3 is used as a project management tool and PDSA (plan, do, study, act) is used in the implementation of

continual improvement. After six months of implementation, clinic revenue rose 10.8%, satisfaction with the
intake process for new patients increased from 63%
to 87%, satisfaction with the number of voicemails
left increased from 38% to 75%, satisfaction with the
authorization process increased from 25% to 74%, satisfaction with the time to answer patient calls increased
from 38% to 75%, patient complaints decreased from
27% to 4%, the rate of failure decreased 42%, and the
rate of billing rejection improved 72%.

In addition to the above steps, there are also steps that can be
used in the context of the central surgical unit. These include:[15]

1. Check the current managerial system to determine activities that add value from the patient's perspective. Here the
   patient must be seen as a process and activity. In addition,
   the team must determine the value based on the patient's
   health problems or potential patients or demographic indicators. Next, the process analysis that takes place in the
   surgical unit should use the SIPOC (supplier, input, process, output, and customer) framework. The supplier here
   is the anesthetist and surgeon; the input is the instruments
   and documents given by the supplier; the process is all
   the logical activities that comprise surgical interventions;
   the output is in the form of documents, maintenance, and
   postoperation inspection; and the customer is the patient
   or medical personnel from other units.
2. Compose a value stream map for the surgical unit. This
   map should include takt time (time between patient
   demand and acceptance of the unit), cycle time (time from
   preoperation to postoperation, respectively split into more
   detailed activities), flow (patient flow and waiting time),
   push (alternative patient flow to avoid failure), and exchange
   time (time to prepare the operating room for surgical intervention). In addition, measurement and evaluation of the

value stream map should be made so that we know what happens, when it happens, and why. Furthermore, a performance index is made for each type of surgery. This index includes operator cycle time (total medical and nonmedical activities on every surgical intervention), activity ratio (percentage of time the activity is actually executed), total surgeries per year, total working hours per year, total medical and nonmedical staff, takt time, cycle time, total medical and nonmedical errors, total medical and nonmedical incidents, waiting time, and supplies. The last step is the future value stream map reprojection, which makes performance targets that will be the improvement target.

3. Implement standardized work and 5S (sorting, organizing, cleaning, standardization, and discipline). Protocols that are not yet available should be created to provide standardized work, which then can become the transformation targets using 5S. These include surgical, infection prevention, linen folding, daily cleaning, sanitary, and aseptic protocols.

4. Implement *poka yoke*. Poka yoke is a technique for quality assurance to eliminate errors. This step is executed by classifying failed surgeries by type of intervention, gender, and age. Error elimination is also done by removing useless procedures, old instruments, damaged material, expired drugs, and human errors that are avoidable through continual learning education (CLE).

5. Implement quick exchange. Quick exchange or SMED (single-minute exchange of die) aims to reduce exchange time by minimizing the amount of work done for a process. This is achieved through a patient hospitalization plan that is carried out in the next few months to anticipate the arrival of the patient again. Also, a surgery program schedule should be made based on routine surgical interventions and the hospitalization of previous patients. This schedule is updated each day by taking into account the various problems that may occur because of an unexpected event.

References

1. Edmonson, A.C. 2003. Framing for Learning: Lessons in Successful Technology Implementation. *California Management Review*, 45(2): 7.
2. Hadi, U., Duerink, D.O., Lestari, E.S., Nagelkerke, N.J., Keuter, M., In't Veld, D.H., Suwandojo, E., Rahardjo, E., van den Broek, P., Gyssens, I.C. 2008. Audit of Antibiotic Prescribing in Two Governmental Teaching Hospital in Indonesia. *Clinical Microbiology and Infection*, 14: 698–707.
3. Radyowijati, A., Haak, H. 2003. Improving Antibiotic Use in Low Income Countries: An Overview of Evidence on Determinants. *Social Science & Medicine*, 57: 733–744.
4. Tvedt, C., Sjetne, I.S., Helgeland, J., Bukholm, G. 2012. A Cross-Sectional Study to Identify Organisational Processes Associated with Nurse-Reported Quality and Patient Safety. *BMJ Open*, 2: e001967.
5. El-Jardali, F., Dimassi, H., Jamal, D., Hemadeh, N. 2011. Predictors and Outcomes of Patient Safety Culture in Hospitals. *BMC Health Services Research*, 11: 45.
6. Tweedy, J.T. 2005. *Healthcare Hazard Control and Safety Management*. 2nd Edition. Boca Raton, FL: Taylor and Francis, p. 695.
7. Aiken, L.H., Clarke, S.P., Cheung, R.B., Silber, J.H. 2003. Educational Levels of Hospital Nurses and Surgical Patient Mortality. *JAMA*, 290: 1617–1623.
8. Scheier, M.F., Matthews, K.A., Owens, J.F., Schulz, R., Bridges, M.W., Magovern, G.J., Carver, C.S. 1999. Optimism and Rehospitalization after Coronary Artery Bypass Graft Surgery. *Archives of Internal Medicine*, 159: 829–835.
9. Johnson, J.E. 2006. Surgery. In *Encyclopedia of Nursing Research*, ed. J.J. Fitzpatrick. 2nd Edition. London: Springer, p. 587.
10. Krishnaiyer, K., Chen, F.F., Kuriger, G. 2011. *Value Stream Mapping: Applied to Health Care Systems—Background and Case Studies*. San Antonio, TX: Center for Advanced Manufacturing and Lean Systems, p. 11.
11. Willis, J. 2007. *Foundations of Qualitative Research: Interpretive and Critical Approaches*. Thousand Oaks, CA: Sage, p. 229.

12. Menachemi, N., Collum, T.H. 2011. Benefits and Drawbacks of Electronic Health Record Systems. *Risk Management and Healthcare Policy*, 4: 47–55.
13. Barnas, K. 2011. ThedaCare's Business Performance System: Sustaining Continuous Daily Improvement through Hospital Management in a Lean Environment. *The Joint Commission Journal on Quality and Patient Safety*, 37(9): 387–399.
14. Niedzwiecki, D., Stanley, J., Anderson, A., Bartels, C., Gonzalez, M., Ibarra, A., Padgett, S., Saffold, B., Wilson, R., Martin, N.A. 2011. *Applying Lean to Improve Resource Utilization and Increase Patient Satisfaction*. San Diego, CA: UCLA Neurosurgery.
15. Viorel, B., Mihaela, C.A. 2009. Lean Hospital—Conceptualization and Instrumentation. In *European Integration—New Challenges for the Romanian Economy International Conference Proceedings*, p. 189.

Chapter 7

Lean Implementation in the Intensive Care Unit

Intensive Care Unit Issues

The ICU is the most dangerous part in the hospital for patients. This is because the ICU is a space that contains many types of germs, which come from the patients themselves. Germs initially strike one patient, but because there are many patients in one room and all are in vulnerable states caused by unhealthy conditions, germs can be transmitted easily. It is no wonder that in South Korea alone, more than 90% of *Staphylococcus aureus* is found in the ICU and causes many infections.[1] When a hospital tries to cope with antibiotics, germs evolve to generate new types of bacteria that are more resistant and therefore more dangerous for patients who take antibiotics, and especially for those who do not take antibiotics.[2] Even worse, all patients and hospital workers, especially medical staff, have the potential to be exposed to materials that have the potential to cause other infections such as blood pathogens; this is due to the nature of ICU, which is immediate and life-saving.[3] About 5% of ICU patients acquire infections just by being in the ICU. The cost borne by hospitals for infections from the hospital itself ranges from $1,000 to $36,000 for each common central infection, and within a year infections cause a $28 billion loss in the United States and result in 99,000 deaths.[4] This is in addition to other exposures, such as latex allergies or exposure to wet surfaces that cause one to slip and fall.[3] This is a form of waste because it lowers the hospital's image as a hotbed of disease and makes revenue decline significantly.

The ICU is also the most overlooked part of the hospital when it comes to patients' desires. This is not bad—and even needed. In contrast to the surgical unit or emergency department, which deal with helpless patients, the ICU has patients who are partially to fully conscious and able to express their wishes.[5] Even so, the surgical, emergency, and ICU units are solid parts of a hospital that are full of knowledge. In other words, all healthcare in the units relies on the results of several years of education and training. In comparison, patients often do not have any experience with their illness or injuries and yet demand to be treated according to their wishes. Of course, the physicians or the nurses know better. Only the medical profession that has the right to determine what is good, fair, serious, critical, and not known in the ICU.[6] This is why when given greater authority to make decisions, nurses in the ICU have increased intrinsic motivation.[7] Medical decision making is exclusively for experts in their field. Trying to appease patients' desires can endanger them and even threaten their lives. Dealing with short-term and long-term patient satisfaction can only be faced by clearly speaking to patients and explaining their condition to them.

The above issue highlights the problem of interpersonal relationships between nurses and physicians and patients and caregivers. But problems in the ICU also occur among physicians. The ICU is similar to the emergency department; both units are filled with specialists who cooperate.[8] This is important because it improves the recovery of patients as well as reduces the death rate and illness severity[9] and lowers the cost per ICU discharge up to 21%.[10] However, because one patient can be treated by several physicians at once, each physician can provide a different medical opinion—and even contradictory ones if they do not cooperate—or insist on their own opinion. Therefore, cooperation among the specialists in the ICU is an issue for this unit.

For nurses, the work in the ICU is also more challenging. The needs of patients continue to change and often must be recognized by the nurses themselves because the patient is unable to communicate them or is in an unstable condition.[11] Nurses also have to think critically in the practical conditions that require immediate and quick actions and decisions.[12] Critical thinking skills are necessary for analyzing complex data on critical patients and making the right decisions in determining appropriate interventions and anticipating the problems that may appear in patients.[11] This is compounded by the poor working physical environment, family problems, and equipment problems.[13]

Both of these issues, the relationship between the patient and medical personnel and relationships among medical personnel, have the potential to cause a wide range of waste, ranging from medication errors to time wasted. Forms of this waste can threaten patients' lives[14] in these kinds of condition, and therefore Lean implementation is required.

Lean Implementation in the Intensive Care Unit

Numerous Lean implementation studies have been done in the intensive care unit—either a specialist unit or a unit based on the severity level—and they have shown good promise. Lean implementation in a Pittsburgh intensive care unit at a general hospital, for example, managed to save the hospital nearly $500,000 per year in ICU fees.[15] Meanwhile, Lean implementation in the neuroscience intensive care unit at the MCG Health System in Augusta, Georgia, is directed toward reducing space waste by using a patient-centered approach. The consideration is that the narrow space actually creates waste because patients become more miserable. Therefore, the hospital decided to redesign the patients' rooms so that family members can stay with them the entire time. This step successfully decreased the medication error rate by up to 62%, reduced staff vacancy from 7.5% to 0%, decreased the length of stay by 50%, and increased patient satisfaction from 10% to 95%.[16] Jimmerson, Weber, and Sobek conducted a study of four units at Intermountain Health Care: a trauma/shock care unit, medical care unit, central surgical unit, and emergency unit.[17] Many results were obtained from this study. Especially for the intensive care unit, improvement was found in the reduction of waste time and medical errors. A problem found by Lean team was that nurses put a glucometer at one intensive care unit, but most of the patients had intensive insulin protocols. As a result, time waste and medical errors occurred. The solution was obvious: put a glucometer in each room of the ICU. This decreased the glucose test time from 17 minutes to four minutes, increased the staff's ability to run the protocol consistently, prevented specimens from going unlabeled, and decreased nurse interruptions and frustration. Some forms of Lean implementation are as simple as this, such as installing new, more satisfactory software[18] or having policies that allow any worker to report to another unit if there are problems, such as at Allegheny General Hospital in Pittsburgh.[19] The solutions seem obvious, but what is difficult is finding the problems, and these problems have been found through Lean techniques.

Let's take a look at the Lean steps undertaken at Allegheny General Hospital:[20]

1. Build policy: There is no problem that should be left unresolved.
2. Ask anyone, whether they are housekeeping employees, health workers, or patients, to report problems to the staff. Staff should also be able to see a problem independently if it is not known to others. The staff report to the leaders of the ICU as well as other officers if there are problems to be solved.

3. One day, two issues were found: First, a patient with a femoral infection was left in the ICU instead of being relocated. Second, there was a problem in the placement procedure of a patient who needed infection care. It was recorded that there were 1,110 patients who received the femoral treatment protocol that had a potential infection, and infection manifested as many as 49 times in 37 patients. The rate of infection was 10.5 infections per 1,000 hospitalization days, resulting in 19 deaths (51%).

4. Two objectives were made, one long-term and the other short-term. The short-term goal was relocation the day after treatment. The long-term goal was no case of infection ever again for anyone.

5. The problem now was to decide who would be responsible for separating patients with an infection when it was discovered. It was concluded that two agents could complete the task: the ICU occupant (doctors, nurses, nurse assistants, cleaning service) and the patient's family. Because the patient's family is not there at night, in the evening the responsibility is handed over to the ICU occupant. The occupants put the patient on a femoral line, and the next day the patient's family transfers the patient from the femoral line.

6. The next problem was determining how the patient's relatives or family would know the patient had been transferred. The solution was to create a tag for the patient and a matching one for the report placed at the patient's bedside. During the night shift, the ICU occupants put both tags in place so that the next day the patient's relatives see them and immediately make the transfer.

7. The patient's family or relatives take the infected patient to the nurse. The nurse makes changes to the materials and methods, such as the equipment used and rapid steam cleaners.

8. During the first year of this procedure, it was found that from 1,321 standard operational procedures with infection risk, only six infections occurred in six patients. The

infection rate was now 1.2 infections per 1,000 hospitalization days, and the death rate was only one patient per
1,000 hospitalization days (16%).

9. In the third year, from 1,898 standard operational procedures
   there were only three infections and three affected patients.
   The infection rate was 0.39 and the death rate 0% per 1,000
   hospitalization days. The hospital saved $1 million per year.

Another lesson can be taken from the ICU at Dominican
Hospital, Santa Cruz County, California.[21] The steps taken were
as follows:

1. Previously, the ICU staff replaced the patient ventilator
   circuit on a daily basis because they felt that this helped
   in the prevention of pneumonia. But after attending an
   ICU conference, they learned that the more often nurses
   handle the ventilator circuit, the higher the chance of
   infection. To minimize nurse contact, a schedule should
   be made and it should be clear whether or not the ventilator circuit has been checked.
2. The staff follow the PDSA (plan, do, study, act) step. To
   indicate that a circuit has been checked, the nurse puts a
   red ribbon on the patient's bed scale. This is a visual clue
   that can be seen from a distance so that the nurses do not
   need to make contact with or check a tool to determine if
   the circuit has been checked.
3. In addition, the staff introduced a list of daily therapy
   goals for each patient. This list tracks their progress
   toward their therapy goals. When created, the list can be
   revised up to 25 times via the PDSA step before a final
   version is used and standardized. Revisions are made so
   that the nurses do not feel that the list adds their workload. In this process, training is done with the frontline
   staff, including listening to input from them. The result of
   this intervention has been a decrease in ventilator use, on
   average from 6.5 to 3.7 in one year of implementation.

4. The staff also received feedback that research has proven that hyperglycemia control helps to reduce death in the ICU. Based on this evidence, the staff designed an intravenous insulin infusion protocol (IV) via the PDSA step. Revisions were carried out eight times before the protocol became standard. As a result of this intervention, the rate of ICU death decreased from 1.2 to 0.4 within six months.

References

1. Pai, C.H. 1999. Antimicrobial Resistance in the Intensive Care Unit. In *Proceedings of the US-Korea Forum on Emerging Infectious Disease*. Arlington, VA: George Mason University School of Law, pp. 104–114.
2. McKenna, M. 2011. The Enemy Within. *Scientific American*, 304(4): 47–53.
3. Tweedy, J.T. 2005. *Healthcare Hazard Control and Safety Management*. 2nd Edition. Boca Raton, FL: Taylor and Francis, p. 411.
4. Klevens, M., Edwards, J.R., Richards, C.L., Horan, T.C., Gaynes, R.P., Pollock, D.A., Cardo, D.M. 2007. Estimating Health Care-Associated Infections and Deaths in US Hospitals, 2002. *Public Health Reports*, 122: 160–166.
5. Ipsos MORI. 2010. *What Do People Want, Need and Expect from Public Services?* London, UK: BBC Trust, p. 44.
6. Mabus, R. 2012. Department of the Navy Public Affairs Policy and Regulations. Washington, DC: SECNAVINST, pp. 2–21.
7. Oudejans, R. 2007. *Linking Extrinsic and Intrinsic Motivation to Job Satisfaction and to Motivational Theories: A Comparison between the Public Sector (Nurses) and the Private Sector (Call Centre Agents)*. Master's thesis, University of Maastricht, p. 68.
8. Klazinga, N.S. 1996. *Quality Management of Medical Specialist Care in the Netherlands: An Explorative Study of Its Nature and Development*. PhD dissertation, Erasmus University, p. 237.
9. Miller, P.A. 2001. Nurse-Physician Collaboration in an Intensive Care Unit. *American Journal of Critical Care*, 10(5): 341–350. See also: Petula, S. 2005. Can Applying Systems Theory Improve Quality in Healthcare Systems? *JHQ*, W6-2–W6-6.

10. Utarini, A., Nugraheni, A.I.P., Agastya, 2009. Improving Clinical Performance: Clinical Management System. In *Hospital Management Training: New Ways to Improve Services in Indonesia*, ed. A. Utarini, G. Schmidt-Ehry, P. Hill. Jakarta, Indonesia: GTZ, p. 171.

11. Kaddoura, M. 2009. *New Graduate Nurses' Perception of Critical Thinking Development in Critical Care Nursing Training Programs.* PhD dissertation, Simmons College Graduate School, p. 3.

12. Wilgis, M., McConnell, J. 2008. Concept Mapping: An Educational Strategy to Improve Graduate Nurses' Critical Thinking Skills during a Hospital Orientation Program. *The Journal of Continuing Education in Nursing*, 39(3): 119–126.

13. Moody, L. 2012. Human Factors and Lean in the ER: A Review of the Literature. In *Symposium on Human Factors and Ergonomics in Health Care*. Baltimore, MD, pp. 20–26.

14. Rosmulder, R.W. 2011. *Improving Healthcare Delivery with Lean Thinking: Action Research in an Emergency Department.* PhD dissertation, University Utrecht, p. 3.

15. Ilin, V., Simic, D., Simic, S. 2012. Lean RFID Approach Enhancing the Information and Material Flows in Emergency Department. *Journal of Medical Informatics and Technologies*, 21: 50.

16. Joint Commission. 2008. Health Care at the Crossroads: Guiding Principles for the Development of the Hospital of the Future. Joint Commission, p. 22.

17. Jimmerson, C., Weber, D., Sobek, D.K. 2004. Reducing Waste and Errors: Piloting Lean Principles at IHC. *Joint Commission Journal on Quality and Safety*, 31(5): 249–257.

18. Kim, S.-C., Horowitz, I., Young, K.K., Buckley, T.A. 2000. Flexible Bed Allocation and Performance in the Intensive Care Unit. *Journal of Operations Management*, 18: 427–443.

19. Lummus, R.R., Vokurka, R.J., Rodeghiero, B. 2006. Improving Quality through Value Stream Mapping: A Case Study of a Physician's Clinic. *Total Quality Management*, 17(8): 1063–1075.

20. Spear, S.J. 2007. *Chasing the Rabbit: What Healthcare Organizations Can Learn from the World's Greatest Organizations.* Cambridge, MA: MIT, pp. 25–30.

21. Berwick, D., Joshi, M.S. 2005. Healthcare Quality and the Patient. In *The Healthcare Quality Book: Vision, Strategy, and Tools*, ed. S.B. Ransom, M.S. Joshi, D.B. Nash. Washington, DC: Aupha, pp. 1–8.

Chapter 8

Lean Implementation in the Radiology Unit

The Waste of the Radiology Unit

Radiology is part of a hospital's most intensive technology, and a standard indicator of this unit relies more on the expertise of the radiologist. A radiology unit must have a high-tech facility in order to continue to survive under pressure that it faces. The existence of this facility is comparable to the service quality so that the financial ability of the hospital will determine how the radiology quality can be improved. When a new technology is introduced in the radiology unit, the social that occurred order is changing. Workers in the radiology unit will try to understand the new tools, and the person with the most expertise will be the most seen in this unit.[1]

The leaning of this unit on technology is actually a gamble. On one hand, the development of rapid demographic gives growth in demand for radiographic imaging services. In addition, the brilliant radiology experts will get great support to grow. Even so, the demand is simply too big to be faced by this unit, especially for hospitals with limited funds. As a result, other parties are trying to provide services. Many physicians from other units have a radiological device and no longer require the assistance of radiology unit. We can now find radiological devices, such as mammography, ultrasound, and so forth, that are not in a radiology unit. There is a possibility that in the future this unit will be completely lost because every other unit in the hospitals has their own devices (Table 8.1).

The physicians in this missing unit can be employed in the unit or do not have work anymore, depending on the complexity of the existing technology. And, unfortunately, technology evolves toward simplification such that untrained people have been able to operate the tools, and radiologists' interpretation is no longer needed. If necessary, the radiologist will be only a support for physicians. The analysis table of five styles below shows the challenges that are faced by radiology units in the future.

The elimination of radiology units can be seen as a Lean step of its own because, if radiology devices are available in every unit or clinic, it will eliminate waste time. Nowadays, for example, orthopedic patients go to the radiology unit before making an appointment with an orthopedic specialist at an outpatient unit. If orthopedic polyclinic has its own bone imaging tool, then the radiology unit is no longer required, and efficiency will occur in terms of waiting time, fees, and the various types of waste associated with it.

Even so, in this book it is assumed that the radiology unit is one of the substantial units in hospitals that should not be removed. So far, many hospitals have radiology units, and it can be expected that 10 years in the future it will still be a central part of the hospital.

Lean Implementation in Radiology Units

Lean implementation in radiology units is generally directed at the reduction of waiting time waste. In addition, the Lean implementation is also done through the use of digital image filing systems, which, at Wilson Memorial Regional Medical

Table 8.1 Forces Affecting the Radiology Unit

Competitor	Potential Competitors	Substitute Products
1. Cardiologist (*peripheral vascular angiography*) 2. Neurologists (CT and MR neurology) 3. Orthopedist (MR orthopedics) 4. Neurosurgery (*neurointerventional radiology*) 5. Medical emergency (radiological emergency) 6. Family practice (chest radiology and musculoskeletal routine)	1. All physicians who own *computer-aided detection* software (mammography) 2. Physician assistant (fluoroscopy procedure) 3. Obstetrics/gynecology (non-*obstetric ultrasonography*) 4. Cardiology (MR cardiac)	1. Progress in computer-aided diagnosis software 2. Breakthrough products in optical imaging, *electron spin resonance* imaging, or other new imaging technology

Buyer	Suppliers	Regulator
1. Referral clinic physician(who order image interpretation) 2. Hospitals, healthcare regional network, and integrated systems (by looking at imaging services providers) 3. Patient 4. Financiers, including the care organizations managed, guarantor, and government program, including JKN (national health insurance).	1. Imaging tools and equipment factory 2. Technology information providers (system communication and picture archiving, applications service providers, digital, technology etc.) 3. Medical schools and academic medical center	1. Central government 2. Regional government

Source: (From Chan, S. 2002. The Importance of Strategy for the Evolving Field of Radiology. *Radiology*, 224: 639–648, p. 644.)

Center, Broome County, New York.[3], resulted in an improved patient output of up to 20% and the reduction of time spent preparing reports by up to 30%. The establishment of a radiology unit network in a health system integrated vertically is capable of producing huge savings in equipment cost.[4]

The following Lean implementation guide departs from a number of implementation studies in a radiology unit:

1. Kaizen cases in a radiology unit at University of Iowa Hospital and Clinics (UIHC)[5]
   a. The formation of cross-functional team. Here, the Lean team consists of 15 people: five radiology specialist, five people who have a general knowledge of radiology, and five from outside of the radiology environment. There are two leadership levels. The first level is the team leader from outside of the radiology environment who understands kaizen approach but does not understand about radiological activity. The second level is the leader of the radiology field as subleader.
   b. First day: The project is started by introducing the Lean concept and doing conceptual training about the processes, methodologies, tools, and Lean techniques. The approach is expected to run 12 hours a day to collect the data and analyze the situation before making suggestions.
   c. Second day: The team is educated about the project, given an understanding of the existing workflow process and the time required to perform process step. In addition, the team is given the understanding of the flow of information and actual travel route to make the process work. In this activity, the activities that add value and do not add value are determined and the ideal workflow is made to reduce activities that do not add value and improve quality. At the end of the activity, the team determines what improvements can be made. The daily activities of the radiology unit are coordinated with

other units in the hospital so that patients and physicians remain accommodated. The team decides to measure the cycle time from the admission of the patients to the scanning room until the next patient enters the scan room. The team is divided into small groups to observe the workflow in three scanners and note the steps required to complete work inspection, as well as the time for each step. After three hours of observation, the team reconvenes to discuss the process and calculate the cycle time. Figure 8.1 shows the workflow that the team finds and a solution offered by the team to eliminate activities that do not add value.

d. Third day: On this day the team evaluates the work-flow in the reception, preparation, and control center areas. They are re-divided to observe areas that are marked and review the previous data. Then they per-form a surgical opinion and develop ideas for process improvements; they also determine and execute the steps required to implement a process improvement plan. Examples of improvements recommended and implemented for the next day are to make faxes of patient information, provide a contrast since the begin-ning, transfer of patient information, IV infusion cover-age, and CT room delivery, as well as the rescheduling of the examination procedure.

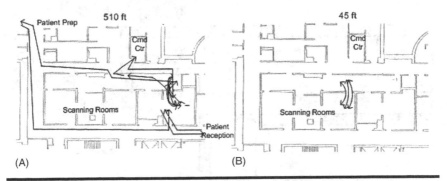

Figure 8.1   (A) Pre-kaizen technologist workflow. (B) Post-kaizen technologist workflow.

e. Fourth day: The examination of implementation preparedness finds obstacles if there are some solutions
that cannot be applied immediately. Therefore, on
this day, the activities are: conduct an actual workplace improvement simulation and evaluate as well as
improve the simulation results. The downside of the
immediate solution is found, and 20 adjustments are
made just for 30 minutes. After that, the implementation is executed again, and at the end of the day, the
staff and patients leave very positive comments. The
team also makes new workflow processes as standard
and prepares to make a report.

f. Fifth day: This is the day where the report is made
and the team celebrates success. The implementation
results are very impressive. There is a reduction of
30% on calls to the command center, a 31% increase
in patient output, a 30% reduction in takt time, a 33%
reduction of total turnaround time (TAT), a 91% reduction in travel time of the technician, and a 50% reduction in travel time of preparation personnel. Figure 8.2
shows the timeline of patients' experience that reduced
from 114 minutes to only 76 minutes. Previously,
patients had to go through three stages: waiting in
reception for preparation for 24 minutes, preparing
to scan for 57 minutes, and scanning for 31 minutes.

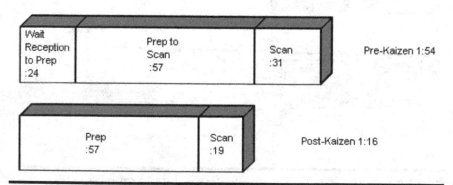

Figure 8.2   Timeline for patient experience.

After implementation, the patient is doing preparation at the same time and the scanning for only 19 minutes. These results allowed the hospital to acquire an additional 3,000 cases and additional revenue of $750,000.

2. Turnaround time cases in the radiology unit of Maimonides Medical Center (MMC) in Brooklyn, New York[6]

   a. The formation of the Department of Labor Management Committee (DLMC). The purpose of this committee is to focus on problem-solving related to services by involving employees in large quantities. Lean is given to the DLMC to ensure they understand the Lean concept. The team followed the Lean steps (see example 1) to identify problems in the radiology unit.

   b. A problem found is a TAT that reaches an average of 25 minutes to find and bring patients from the emergency unit to the radiology unit. As a result, time for X-ray procedures decreases.

   c. The purpose of the team is to reduce the transport time to 15 minutes. To achieve this goal, the DLMC makes the patient turnaround transport team (PT3) whose job is to analyze and advise changes in the flow of patients and work staff to achieve the 10–15-minute target. The DLMC then works for other units in the hospital.

   d. PT3 consults with all employees at the emergency and radiology units to develop and propose a better system in finding and bringing the patient to the X-ray machine. Analysis shows the need for new positions, such as Imager Assistant, that are responsible for bringing the patient whenever needed, ensuring the procedure room is clean, and ensuring that the film and X-ray chart are up-to-date and complete. The team reports this change to the DLMC and gets support for change. As a result, two full-time and one part-time Imager Assistants are employed. The result of this intervention is the reduction of TAT time by up to 40%, from 25 minutes to only 10 minutes.

3. Lean cases of Columbus Regional Hospital (CRH)[7]
   a. CRH's leadership makes a plan to apply Lean imple-
      mentation on four radiology sections: CT, MRI, and
      ultrasound. Each section has its own team. Success is
      measured by the reduction of cycle time, waiting time,
      and capacity. All teams follow the DMAIC (Define,
      Measure, Analyze, Improve, Control) approach. The
      details of these steps include:
      i. Define: Understand the current conditions by look-
         ing at the patients and physician revenue, mapping
         the processes, and finding failure risk.
      ii. Measure: Understand the process through reliable
          metrics and detailed mapping; find processes that
          add value and do not add value, and understand
          the request trace.
      iii. Analyze: Select the critical factors that have the
           most influence on performance, understand the
           content of the work, find waste by Lean tools (value
           analysis, overall equipment effectiveness, spaghetti
           mapping, and setup reduction analysis)
      iv. Improve: Select the best solution for improvement,
          dispose of unnecessary step in the process, give
          the task to staff, create standardized work, train the
          staff, and organize the workplace.
      v. Control: Communicate the changes, make per-
         formance reports, make changes of new ways of
         working, follow-up and verification.
   b. Improvement steps undertaken in CT project, among others:
      i. Move work which is not imaging out of the CT
         room so that it is used only for procedures.
      ii. Give direction package for patients to complete the
          registration.
      iii. Give an incentive to patients if they register by phone.
      iv. Increase coordination between the central schedul-
          ing and telephone registration.
      v. Extend service hours.

c. The result of this procedure is a reduction of 38% at the inspection time, a reduction of 85% in the examination time variation, a 21% increase in patient volume, and a 33.8% increase in revenue.

d. Corrective steps undertaken in ultrasound projects, among others:
    i. Cross training to all technicians for ultrasound and vascular examination.
    ii. Change the examination schedule to the room rather than to technicians.
    iii. Add and update a list of common questions regarding scheduling.
    iv. Implement kit procedures for inspection and inventory improvement using a pull system.
    v. Make a call procedure to remind patients about examination timetable.
    vi. Extend service time.

e. The result of this implementation is an increase in relative value unit (RVU) per hour by 29.6% and 10.1% increase in revenue.

f. Improvement steps for the MRI project, among others:
    i. Redesign of the block schedule and MRI booking forms.
    ii. Add questions of metastatic disease for all MRIs.
    iii. Extend service time.
    iv. Scheduling of trained center to remind the physicians to use a new MRI form, remind the patient to go to the lab before the procedure, and remind the patients to pre-register by phone.
    v. Coordinate with marketing to explain the changes in the physicians' office and communities.
    vi. The result of this implementation is an increase in revenue of 14.3% and a volume increase of 10.1%.

References

1. Barley, S.R. 1986. Technology as an Occasion for Structuring: Evidence from Observations of CT Scanners and Social Order of Radiology Units. *Administrative Science Quarterly,* 31: 24–60. See too Barley, S.R. 1990. The Alignment of Technology and Structure Through Roles and Networks. *Administrative Science Quarterly,* 35: 61–103 and Argote, L., Greve, H.R. 2007. A Behavioral Theory of the Firm—40 Years and Counting: Introduction and Impact. *Organization Science,* 18(3): 337–349, p. 343.
2. Chan, S. 2002. The Importance of Strategy for the Evolving Field of Radiology. *Radiology,* 224: 639–648, p. 644.
3. Ramakrishnan, S., Nagarkar, K., DeGennaro, M., Srihari, M., Courtney, A.K., Emick, F. 2004. A Study of the CT Scan Area of a Healthcare Provider. Paper read at Winter Simulation Conference: Proceedings of the 36th conference on Winter simulation. See also: Hong, T.S., Shang, P.P., Arumugam, M., Mohd Yusuff, R. 2013. Use of Simulation to Solve Outpatient Clinic Problems: A Review of the Literature. *South African Journal of Industrial Engineering,* 24(3): 27–42, p. 35.
4. Lin, B.Y.. 2007. Integration in Primary Community Care Networks (PCCNs): Examination of Governance, Clinical, Marketing, Financial, and Information Infrastructures in a National Demonstration Project in Taiwan. *BMC Health Services Research,* 7: 90, p. 6.
5. Bahensky, J.A., Roe, J., Bolton, R. 2005. Lean Sigma – Will It Work for Healthcare? *Journal of Healthcare Information Management,* 19(1): 39–44.
6. MMC. 2007. *Creating Competitive Advantage in a Changing Health Care Environment Through Worker Participation.* MMC. Retrieved from: https://www.ilr.cornell.edu/sites/ilr.cornell.edu/files/Maimonides%20Report.pdf.
7. SBTI. 2010. *Radiology Improved Processes, Reduced Procedure Time, and Increased Volume and Revenue.* San Marcos, TX: SBTI.

Chapter 9

Lean Implementation in the Clinical Pathology Unit

Clinical Pathology Unit Issues

The clinical pathology unit is more or less the same as the radiology department because it relies on the laboratory and methods such as molecular microbiology. This is where the samples are examined to determine the patient's disease. The main problem in this unit is the reduction in technical staff, the increasing number of test menus, complaints about work-related stress, and room limitations.[1] They continue to feel pressure to work faster, use a minimum of resources, but produce better results.[2]

Lean implementation in clinical pathology units has been done many times. [1-3] DSI Lab, which uses Lean, managed to save more than $400,000 in the first year.[4] A study conducted in Bradford, England, in 2008 managed to prevent unnecessary tests and make sure that people know what type of test is needed and when to ask.[5] Implementation in Bolton, England, resulted in a 70% reduction of total steps needed to complete most of the work, a 40% reduction in floor space required, and a reduction of 90% on time needed to do work.[6] These results are associated with the 10% increase in revenue and a 2% decrease in staff.[7]

Lean Case Studies in Clinical Pathology Units

A study by Persoon et al. in a clinical pathology unit focuses on the problem of turnaround time that occurred in this lab, especially in chemical tests.[2] The customers complain that the turnaround time is too long and therefore needs to be shortened. During this time, the complaints are dealt with in an accelerated process. The problem is the acceleration of the test will result in further chaos because there will be more processes and pathways that complicate the problems. Lean steps are used to solve this problem, among others:

1. Researchers conduct a study of the basic cycle time as a baseline study. Researchers also make performance indexes as well as the purpose. The purpose of Lean implementation is able to report 80% of all chemical tests in less than one hour. If this is done, the process does not need to be accelerated again.
2. Researchers make a process map which describes the line to see the processes that are considered a waste, not necessary, and anything inappropriate. Researchers find that there are two lines, which are regular test and accelerated test. Accelerated test does need not to pass the queue as regular test. But because 40% of the tests are accelerated type, then the accelerated test also goes through the queue and the differences between both tests do not have meaning.
3. Researchers then redesign the process map so that it becomes simpler. This redesign uses Lean steps; some of them are:
    a. One-piece flow. In this step, a sample is completed before another sample is done. There is no distinction between the regular and accelerated. When one

reservation comes, the lab handles all tests and labels
all containers from the booking. Only after this is completed are the containers sorted based on the next process or destination. In other words, the first that enters
is the first that exits. Previously, the sample was sorted
first by priority and labeled separately, so when the
test stage is completed, the label should be re-matched
since much misplacement happens.

b. All work must be very specific based on the content,
sequence, time, and result. For example, samples that
require centrifugation loaded in the centrifuges bucket
in a specific pattern. Rotation is made every 6 minutes,
no matter how many samples or queues. When the
round is completed, the tube that does not require
aliquot is removed and put on the transport shelf.
The tubes that require aliquot are transferred from the
bucket one by one, and then aliquot is given in a tube
without a label. When the tubes are empty, they are
returned to the loading point.

c. Every customer–supplier connection must be direct,
and there should be no ambiguous way to request or
receive a response. If the request does not have complete information, the tester gives a special ticket that
registers what information is lacking, pastes it into the
sample, and puts it in the basket. The laboratory staff
take a special sample and hands it to the exception
handlers. They solve the problem of lack of data, mark
the ticket, and return it back to the tester to start the test
process. Earlier, if there was an incomplete sample, the
process was delayed, and then the tester contacted
the sample source to request the missing information.

d. The line for every product and service must be simple
and direct. The laboratory staff send samples that have
been tested from the tester to centrifuge machines and
send samples that had been rotated directly into chem-
istry loader analyzer. Previously, the samples that had

been processed were stored on the shelf and sent to
the analyzer machine when there were officers who
had spare time or when the laboratory assistant who
worked in the analyzer machine came to take it.

e. Any improvement must be made according to the
scientific method, in counselor's guidance, at the lowest level of organization. Laboratory staff who want to
provide feedback should provide ideas to the supervisors or process engineer. An experiment is designed to
test the idea, and if it is proved to be better, then it is
used as a new standard.

The results of this intervention are the turnaround time is
reduced from an average of 29 minutes to 19 minutes and the
lab achieves the reporting target of 80%; chemical test result
is less than one hour for 11 consecutive months since the
implementation.

Melanson uses a similar approach to a phlebotomy laboratory at Brigham and Women's Hospital.[1] The steps used include:

1. Provide training to the lab staff.
2. Create a committee consisting of trained lab staff plus
   Lean special practitioners. The committee is asked to
   determine the objectives and scope of Lean activities.
3. Ensure that other units help in real time if there are technical and operational changes.
4. Personnel are selected from staff, and their schedules are
   adjusted to make them dedicated to the process.
5. The processes are examined from patient entry to exit from
   the phlebotomy location. Each stage is observed to understand the causes of delay or extension of patient visits.
   Metrics that are collected include patient volume per hour
   and day of the week, staff based on the hour and day of the
   week, and the patient waiting time. Patient waiting time is
   measured at the peak times. Patient satisfaction is measured.
   The result is a 56% better response. Patient dissatisfaction

appears when they are given less information about waiting time. The average waiting time is 21 minutes. The cause of the problem is (i) non blood–related activity decreases the amount of time that can be given to patients by the phlebotomist, (ii) patients are not aware of their position in the queue so that the staff have difficulty in finding patients when their turn comes in the queue, and (iii) many patients come before the lab opens, resulting in the accumulation of the beginning time, which increases the waiting time.

6. The committee conducts an analysis to find improvement solutions. Improvement steps that are done are the removal of activities that do not add to the value, for example, the examination of samples twice before being sent and the use of the log to record when the canister is sent through the pneumatic tube to a lab. The use of stat or rush stickers on all tubes is discarded, and they are only taped to the outside pockets. Previously, the patients could only register with a new registration card and now the expired registration card is also permitted. Answering the phone for common questions is replaced by voicemail. Moreover, an activity of calling transport center for specimens that are not sent by pneumatic tube is replaced with a regular taking by the transport center to avoid phone calls. Patients who are unsure of their place in the queue become sure by the mark of queue serial numbers and a queue number signboard.

7. The result of this implementation is the reduction of the waiting time from 21 minutes to five minutes, patient satisfaction increased by 86%, and 90% of patients get blood samples within 10 minutes of arrival.

The following overview of Bolton Hospital can also be an idea to implement Lean at the clinical pathology unit.[6]

1. The team follows the journey of the blood samples from being taken from the patient to the return to the patient. The movable samples from patients are going toward

hematology, biochemistry, microbiology, and then back again. Every move is tracked and recorded, including the administration steps.

2. A number of improvement steps carried out after the existence of much waste is discovered in the course of the blood sample. The improvement steps, among others, are:

    a. Connect the rooms so the staff can go directly to the next room without passing through the corridor.

    b. Place the analyzers in one place so that the staff does not have to go up and down the stairs to reach it.

    c. Move the central samples reception point from the front to the middle of the unit so that the course of the sample is shorter.

    d. Create a standard form that can be scanned by a computer so that writing and reading time are reduced.

    e. Analyze each rack as soon as it is charged rather than waiting for it to fill.

3. The result of this implementation is awesome. The course of regular blood samples is reduced from initially 309 steps to 57 steps. The emergency blood sample step is reduced from 75 steps to 57 steps, too. Staff mileage to walk is reduced by 80%. Sample course time from the endocrinology and hematinic declines from 24 to 30 hours to just two to three hours. The actual space used by the unit declines to 50%.

References

1. Melanson, S., Goonan, E., Lobo, M., Baum, J., Paredes, J., Santos, K., Gustajson, M., Tanasijevic, M. 2009. Applying Lean/Toyota Production System Principles to Improve Phlebotomy Patient Satisfaction and Workflow. *American Journal of Clinical Pathology*, 132: 914–919.

2. Persoon T., Zaleski, S., Frerichs, J. 2006. Improving Preanalytic Processes Using the Principles of Lean Production (Toyota Production System). *American Journal of Clinical Pathology*, 125(1): 16–25.
3. Zito J.S., Stewart, D.A. 2008. Lean Deploys at Centrex Clinical Labs. *Medical Laboratory Observer*, 40: 32–34.
4. Yeh, H-L., Lin, C-S., Su, C-T., Wang, P-C. 2011. Applying Lean Six Sigma to Improve Healthcare: An Empirical Study. *African Journal of Business Management*, 5(31): 12356–12370.
5. Nasiri, S.D. 2009. *Lean Thinking and Queue Modelling in Healthcare*. Lancaster University Management School, p. 14. Retrieved from: http://www.leadingedgegroup.com/assets/ uploads/Lean_Thinking_and_Queue_Modelling_in_Healthcare. pdf.
6. Jones, D., Mitchell, A. 2006. Lean Thinking for the NHS. An NHS Confederation Leading Edge Report, ISBN 1 85947 127 7. See also Faull, N. 2007. Lean Healthcare: Learning via Action Research. *POMS 18th Annual Conference Dallas*, Texas, May 4–7, 2007, p. 4.
7. Fillingham, D. 2007. Can Lean Save Lives? *Leadership in Health Services*, 20(4): 231–241.

Chapter 10

Lean Implementation in the Pharmaceutical Unit

The pharmaceutical unit is responsible for providing all the prescribed drugs and advising patients about the use of the medication.[1] This unit is important for the hospital economically because 4%–50% of hospital revenue comes from it.[2] It also plays a key role in preventing medication errors, so every worker should understand the importance of safety, the dangers that can be found in the process and work, their role in the event of an emergency, and policies and safety procedures in general.[3] In addition, sometimes a pharmacy unit representative is needed to commit to a cross-disciplinary team for specific tasks such as stroke response and other diseases that are considered as emergency.[4]

Problems faced by pharmaceutical unit and solutions include:

Waste of Time Issues

In terms of waste of time, the pharmaceutical unit has problems. Various attempts have been made to eliminate or decrease waste of time going on in the pharmaceutical unit. One early effort is the use of a queuing system that focuses on priorities, so that orders from the patient are assessed based on the emergency level and the most urgent orders will be prioritized first.[5] In the Lean effort, waste of time can be reduced with a streamlined process developed through process mapping.[6]

Unavailability of Drugs Issues

In terms of drugs, there are two problems that arise: the drugs that are not provided and the existence of expired drugs. Factors that cause this problem can be either external factors such as there is no raw substance, changes in formulation or manufacturing, the difficulty of manufacturing and legislation policy issues, as well as increased demand and changes in clinical practice that are unexpected (see Figure 10.1).[7]

The following template shows a solution to overcome the unavailability of drugs issues at the pharmacy. In general, the steps that should be done after a drug shortage condition is found are to conduct operational and therapist assessments. After that, the next step is to analyze the impact of drug shortages. After the impact analysis is done, the next step is making a final plan, and then it is communicated and implemented. These steps can be run by the pharmaceutical unit or special teams.

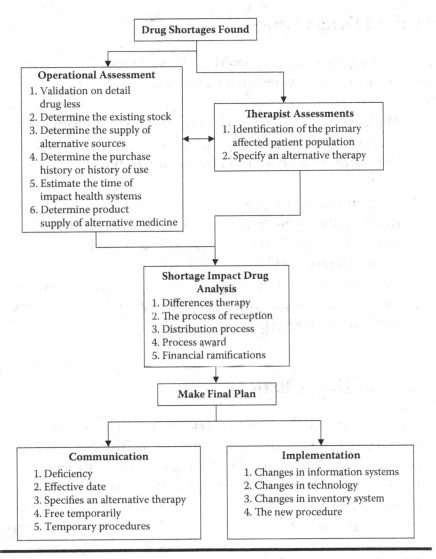

Figure 10.1 Mechanisms to overcome drug shortage. (From Fox, E.R., Birt, A., James, K.B., Kokko, H., Salverson, S., Sofli, D.I. 2009. ASHP Guidelines on Managing Drug Product Shortages in Hospitals and Health Systems. *American Journal of Health-System Pharmacy,* **66: 1399–406.)**

Expired Drugs Issues

Expired drugs issues are related to the drug supply management system. This management includes:[2]

1. The development of a drug formulary. A drug formulary is needed for drug supply management and should therefore be developed and led by the medical committee of the hospital.
2. Determination of target supply level. The intended target supply is the appropriate drug supply level. If there are too many available drugs, there will be a higher possibility that expiry will happen.
3. Determination of safe supply level. A safe supply level is the minimum drug supply level that still ensures that service level is reached.

Waste of Drugs Issues

Other issues may include medication errors such as drugs lost, wasted, or returned from the patient's room. These are Lean problems because they are directly related to the waste of drugs that already exist. Lean implementation has been run in pharmaceutical units, for example, at Musgrove Park Hospital, Somerset, England.[8] This hospital uses process and value mapping, capacity estimation, effects analysis of failure process mode to reduce waste of time and improve patient and nurse satisfaction. The implementation results are quite satisfactory because the time of drug dispensing from ordering to accepting is down from 188 minutes to 27 minutes and is continual. Because of this efficiency, the daily works have been completed 65% before 1 p.m. and closed at 5.30 p.m. Although the rate of medication errors does not change, this intervention has been enough to reduce the dispense time without increasing the workload of staff and harming the patient.

The rate of medication errors alone can be reduced by ordering using electronic systems such as e-mail.[9] Pharmacy Management System (PMS), for example, allows the *pharmaceutical* workers to enter and fill physician orders and perform all the functions related to patients' billing, drug inventory updates, re-supply schedule, and inventory care. The advantages of PMS are its ability to automatically check interactions among drugs, drugs and food, and any contraindication allergies that may arise; this is useful for informing patients and caregivers about what not to do when using drugs.[10]

Other inventory waste reduction cases can be emulated from RS Exempla.[11] In the initial conditions, there are three drug dispenser machines in the pharmaceutical unit which are all located away from patient care areas. Each machine has a different inventory of and is difficult to manage. Drugs there also look the same or sound the same when stored adjacent to one another inside the machine, so it can lead to medication errors. Moreover, there is no way of knowing which machines have the drugs needed by the nurse.

In these circumstances, the hospital needs to establish a process which can distinguish drugs with a higher risk in the dispenser machine. In addition, the hospital needs to determine inventory needs based on the usage, thereby reducing the inventory waste. Moreover, the hospital also needs to evaluate the overall medication standard and improve the care efficiency by redesigning the drug dispenser machine location.

What is conducted then by RS Exempla? After going through the value mapping process, the Lean team decides to perform six steps. First, they move the dispenser machine into a separate room so that it is easy to find. Furthermore, they standardize the work for drug dispenser machine maintenance and use only one drug dispenser machine. Other than that, the inventories are modified to suit the needs of the patient by eliminating the unused drug excess. Meanwhile, drug delivery time to drug dispenser machine is standardized, and the time until drugs are available to be given is also lowered. Waste of motion is lowered by reducing the distance that must be taken by nurses to get to the drug dispenser machine.

The results of this intervention are the pharmaceutical unit only has one drug dispenser machine, which saves up to $7,887.33 in inventory costs. In three days, the total drugs sent to the intensive care unit (ICU) decreased by 28% and the number of drugs in the dispenser machine that were not used decreased 62%, from 362 drugs to 136 drugs.

Waste of Space Issues

The hospital pharmacy at Cincinnati Children's Hospital provides examples on how Lean is used to overcome the waste of space issues.[11] The pharmaceutical unit in this hospital was problematic because of inefficient workspace, the loss and waste of many drugs, drugs returned from the patients' rooms, and the long time of the drug dispensing process.

A Lean consultant is hired and a Lean team created and assigned to observe the processes and workflow of pharmaceutical workers in a regular workday. This observation results in several findings related to waste causes. For example, the team finds that the lab room is used inefficiently and therefore they ask for advice from the pharmaceutical workers about how these problems can be solved. The pharmaceutical workers said that there is a need for new shelves to make the workspace neat and reliable. This team soon calls the maintenance staff to make contemporary shelves in the pharmacy and observe whether the presence of the shelves has a positive impact on the workspace. The observations find that the shelves indeed have a positive impact and, hence, the shelves are made permanent.

This is just one example of the Lean steps performed by the Lean consultant and team. Overall, the process undertaken gets results of 50% reduction of the returned drugs from the patients' rooms. In addition, there is a reduction of 58% on the mileage of pharmaceutical workers, a 43% increase in workspace, and a reduction of 75% on process time, so a one-day job turns out to be only five hours.

It should be noted that Lean can also be a negative impact on workers in a pharmaceutical unit. Lean demands change, and workers tend to not want to take risks by making changes if such changes could potentially produce the worst effects, such as loss of job due to inability to adapt. The changes brought by Lean on pharmaceutical workers can be changes of physical location and job description.[11] If, of the Lean staff, only a few compare to the existing staff, a social jealousy and suspicion will present on why certain staff members are selected while others not.[11] This indicates a failure to involve all personnel in the unit, including non-pharmaceutical personnel.[12] This will lower the staff spirit. Therefore, interventions are required through extensive communication.

References

1. Folinas, D., Faruna, T. 2011. Implementing Lean Thinking Paradigm Practices in Medical Set Up. *Business Management Dynamics*, 1(2): 61–78.
2. Utarini, A., Nugraheni, A.I.P., Agastya, 2009. Improving Clinical Performance: Clinical Management System. In *Hospital Management Training: New Ways to Improve Services in Indonesia*. Jakarta, Indonesia: GTZ, p. 194.
3. Tweedy, J.T. 2005. *Healthcare Hazard Control and Safety Management*. 2nd Edition. Boca Raton, FL: CRC Press, p. 483.
4. Korobey, M.J., Crannage, A.J., Murphy, J.A., Jensen, J.M., Hipsky, B.J. 2011. Pharmacy Department Commitment to a Multidisciplinary Stroke Response Team. *American College of Clinical Pharmacy*, Annual Meeting, Pittsburgh, PA, October 2011; Lanham, K., Cangany, L.S. Clinical Pharmacy Technicians: Impact in Cardiology and Critical Care Pharmacy Services. *American College of Clinical Pharmacy*, Annual

Meeting, Pittsburgh, PA, October 2011; Lyons, K.M., Bohn, S. A. Mentoring Program for Clinical and Operation Supervisors. *American College of Clinical Pharmacy*, Annual Meeting, Pittsburgh, PA, October 2011.

5. Fomundam, S., Hermann, J. 2007. A Survey of Queuing Theory Applications in Healthcare. *ISR Technical Report* 2007–24, p. 11.

6. NHS Institute for Innovation and Improvement. 2008. Lean in Hereford. Retrieved from: www.institute.nhs.uk/quality_and_va lue/lean_thinking/leean_case_studies.html.

7. Fox, E.R., Birt, A., James, K.B., Kokko, H., Salverson, S., Sofli, D.I. 2009. ASHP Guidelines on Managing Drug Product Shortages in Hospitals and Health Systems. *American Journal of Health-System Pharmacy*, 66: 1399–406.

8. Beard, J., Wood, D. 2010. Application of Lean Principles can Reduce Prescription Dispensing Times. *Pharmaceutical Journal*, 284/7597(369–371): 0031–6873.

9. Silow-Carroll, S., Alteras, T., Meyer, J.A. 2007. Hospital Quality Improvement: Strategies and Lessons from US Hospitals. *The Commonwealth Fund Report*, 54, p. 36.

10. Angst, C.M. 2007. *Information Technology and Its Transformational Effect on the Health Care Industry*. PhD dissertation, University of Maryland, p. 161.

11. Hines, S., Luna, K., Lofthus, J., Stelmokas, D. 2008. Becoming a High Reliability Organization: Operational Advice for Hospital Leaders. (Prepared by the Lewin Group under Contract No. 290-04-0011.) *AHRQ Publication* No. 08-0022. Rockville, MD: Agency for Healthcare Research and Quality. April 2008, p. 54.

12. Shortell, S.M., Bennett, C.L., Byck, G.R. 1998. Assessing the Impact of Continuous Quality Improvement on Clinical Practice: What It Will Take to Accelerate Progress. *The Milbank Quarterly*, 76(4): 593–614, p. 598.

Chapter 11

Lean Implementation in the Nutrition Unit

Nutrition Unit Issues

The nutrition unit in a hospital works to provide nutritional consultation and catering diets that are required by patients in order to meet nutritional needs. The relationship of this unit is closely related to the inpatient unit since it provides nutrition for patients treated in the inpatient unit. In addition, for the hospitals that have a gynecology unit, the unit is needed to prepare infant or pregnant mothers' formula. Moreover, this unit is also responsible for maintaining food safety in hospitals as a whole.

The common problem faced by this unit is the outreach and, of course, the waiting time. A patient cannot get food for a day if the nutrition unit performs poorly, especially in terms of information and communication between members or units. Similarly, patients can wait long if the officers must spend too much time traveling to bring food. In the case of the Prince of Wales Hospital, the nutrition unit has separate systems for the production, scheduling, and delivery of food which relies on patient data that is often too late to enter in the hospital information system; as a result, it is difficult to find patients and food is wasted.[1] This often happens so that the workers at the nutrition unit, in addition to being good at nutrient management, should also be proficient in negotiating and delegation.[2]

Part of the nutrition unit issues can be solved by using a better information system. Recipe storage software for specific patients, for example, will greatly assist in dispensing the proper food for patients. Lean application in nutrition units can come just at the product design. Burlodge is a brand of food service equipment products, including food service in hospitals. Burlodge implements Lean implementation on food service furniture design that they call B-Lean. B-Lean is a product designed to be highly adaptive. B-Lean contains a system which consists of several different components designed in such a way as to create work cells that are in line with the background. In this system, the packaging, cleaning, and actuating of individual parts process becomes very easy. The design that is in line with the human workflow ensures everything needed to make food preparation in the hospital easy to access, move, and carry out. A gravity system helps the basket scroll the table, lowering the container and food shelves to be easily accessed, and move in tight spaces. It is claimed that the B-Lean design saves a time of 30%–40% on food preparation and improves patient satisfaction scores.[3]

Lean Case Studies in Nutrition Units

Many efforts made for Lean implementation in the nutrition unit are particular in the sense that they only address certain aspects of the nutrition unit task. In Adelaide Community Healthcare Alliance (ACHA) Hospital, in Australia, for example, an aspect that becomes the implementation target is patient satisfaction on food.[4] The steps undertaken by the ACHA Hospital are as follows.

1. Periodic surveys of patient satisfaction are conducted on the patients who are treated and patients who have been discharged from the hospital.
2. From the results of this survey, the investigators adjust the nutritional needs and the results of the survey so that the most beneficial food menu from both sides is found. Adjustments are made through software that performs nutritional analysis and chooses the most optimal food in satisfying the patient.
3. A team is formed to assess the steps taken through consultation of quality improvement. In addition to assessing the food in terms of nutritional needs and consumer satisfaction, the team also provides other suggestions to reduce waste.
4. Team and workers continue to monitor incidents and carry out an evaluation of clinical risk management. If there is a new idea, this idea is discussed collaboratively.

The result of the implementation is the increase in patient satisfaction from the menu selection, food quality, and overall satisfaction by an average of 55%.

The Peter MacCallum Cancer Centre in Australia conducts a Lean project to develop sustainable training and mentoring for nutritional workers in the management of head, neck and upper gastrointestinal cancers. A sustainable plan is developed and implemented to maintain and build the knowledge, attitude, and confidence of nutritional workers. This system is not directed directly toward the solving problem but at an early stage to address the problems that may occur in the future. It includes an initial survey of patients from various backgrounds and involvement of the patients' perspectives in care steps they need from a nutrition perspective.[5] Something different is the involvement of the nutrition unit in the team, which therefore provides a richer perspective on the problems faced by patients. Similar steps are done to address malnutrition problems in the same hospital using the new malnutrition screening tool, which is more reliable.[6] Other implementation can be directed to the aspects of food dispensing by using food providers and retail that meet ISO 22000 standards on the Food Safety Management System.[7]

Various Lean implementations mentioned previously follow a Lean implementation model called the Evaluation and Quality Improvement Program (EQuIP). EQuIP was developed by the Australian Council on Healthcare Standards (ACHS), an independent non-profit corporation started in 1974 by a group of industrial organizations, consumers, governments, and academics in Australia.[8] This principle is actually one of the sources for the development of the Komisi Akredirasi Rumah Sakit (KARS) accreditation system in Indonesia in 1995. EQuIP consists of five principles:

1. Consumer focus: Steps should be directed at consumers by involving the patients as a source, involved in the process, and getting results. As a source, the patient can be involved in the form of questionnaires or interviews regarding the aspects that need improvement. Involvement in the process can be seen from how patients are included, for example, in decision making. Involving of the patients in the results is shown in the indicators that show improvement in the patient.
2. Effective leadership: Steps must have strong leadership in organizing and directing the program on objectives outlined.
3. Continuous improvement: There should be steps undertaken continuously to ensure that the quality is maintained and, if possible, increased.
4. Evidence of results: This principle requires evidence of successful implementation from the patient side as well as the unit side.
5. Endeavor becomes the best practice: This principle outlines the importance of successful implementation deployed on various other units or nutrition units in other hospitals so that they can solve similar problems that are faced.

References

1. Brayan, D.J. 2005. *Using Technology for Bed Management in Public Hospitals – A Strategic Analysis and Change Management Plan.* Master's thesis, Simon Fraser University, p. 43.
2. Noble, B.C.L. 1976. *Identification of Tasks Performed by United States Army Dietitians Which Are Perceived as Delegable to Enlisted Personnel Having the 94F50 or 94F40 Military Occupational Specialty.* PhD dissertation, George Washington University, p. 48.
3. Burlodge. 2013. *Lean Thinking Drives Burlodge: The Serious Savings Behind Improved Ergonomics and Efficiencies, Dishing it Up!* 3, p. 39.
4. Harman, K., Moore, C. 2011. Meeting the Nutritional Needs of the Patient Safely: Adelaide Community Healthcare Alliance Incorporated (ACHA HEALTH), ACHA Hospitals Diet Working Party, SA. *14th Annual ACHS Quality Improvement Awards*, pp. 22–23.
5. Hamilton-Keene, R., Kiss, N., Moylan, R. 2011. Improving Care for Regional Cancer Patients through Collaboration between Integrated Cancer Services to Support and Mentor Regional Health Professionals. *14th Annual ACHS Quality Improvement Awards*, pp. 38–40.
6. Loeliger, J., Hodgson, B., Barrington, V., Retemeyer, D., Cuttriss, T. 2011. Malnutrition Inpatient Strategy. *14th Annual ACHS Quality Improvement Awards*, pp. 123–125.
7. Bambry, D. 2011. Supply Safe Food, or Don't Supply at All!! *14th Annual ACHS Quality Improvement Awards*, pp. 215–216.
8. Hort, K., Djasri, H., Utarini, A. 2013. *Regulating the Quality of Health Care: Lessons from Hospital Accreditation in Australia and Indonesia.* Melbourne: Nossal Institute for Global Health, p. 7.

Chapter 12

Lean Implementation in the Medical Record Unit

Medical Record Unit Issues

As well as the radiology department, the medical record unit is an endangered unit due to the development of information technology, which allows each core unit to have access to electronic medical records and no longer requires the medical record unit. It is a traditional unit that stores the patient data from the entire history of the hospital in offline form. This traditional method is actually not good for the financial health of the hospital. Medical records that build up too fast can overpower the human resources available so that hospitals can lose income because most medical records could not be converted into a bill for the patients. In other words, manual labor is too big; electronic work may also be too big if the electronic design is still too rough and the speed of data entry is slower than the speed of manual writing.[1]

Of all hospital parts, the medical record unit is the most antique unit in the sense of having medical records of patients that span from the time the hospital was first established. This information can be valuable, and many other units also consider it important for particular patients' medical record information. Problems related to the seizing of medical record documents often occur between the medical record unit and other units, fighting over particular patients' medical record documents because of the high value, especially in terms of finance. The unit may favor the patient, so it does not want to hand over the documents to the medical record unit and therefore reduce the function of such a unit for those who do not understand the existence of this internal conflict. In addition, at very old hospitals, a number of medical record documents become extremely valuable because of their age and association with famous figures who have got treatment at the hospital. The documents are often guarded and are not included in the computer system.[1]

The most common waste for the medical record unit is the waiting time associated with processing time at the unit. In the very traditional system, an officer must examine piles of data for obtaining the patient data. When the data is not accurate, for example, because a patient has the same name as another patient, there will be difficulties in access that lengthen the waiting time. Usually, when patients order a place in the hospital, the medical records officer will check the patient's medical records and hand it to the physician to review and, based on their advice, the patients are given the right place at the hospital. This process can take from five minutes up to 36 days.[2]

Lean implementation in this unit can be illustrated with the following examples from National Health Service (NHS) hospitals in the United Kingdom.[2] An NHS hospital has a problem of delay and cancellation due to the inefficient flow of patients' medical records. A Lean implementation technique is run involving three units at once: the medical record unit, the inpatient unit, and medical secretaries. The Lean team formed consists of a group of managers, secretaries, employees, and nurses. The team is trained in the Lean principles.

The first step taken by the Lean team is to build an information flow map. This map illustrates from when the patients pose a health problem to when they are released. The mapping results are quite surprising. A patient, on average, has to pass more than 150 procedures and 50 replacement handling responsibilities. There being so many steps is one reason for the inefficiency of the medical record services. In addition to excessive steps, a problem found is poor communication between the units. The Lean team focuses on efforts to remove procedures that do not add value and which, in fact, add to the cost and the time to respond to the patient.

Steps taken by the Lean team in the context of medical records are to create standard letters and forms, redesign the layout, mark files in the library so that they can be easier and faster to find, and shorten the distance between employee desks and the printer. Empty space is created in which to store predicted patients' medical records the day before their arrival. This step generates savings of 57 hours per week. Standard letters and forms are submitted to the secretaries and they hire one additional officer for help. The additional officer enables the unit to handle the previously piling work. Standard letters and forms prevent new work from accumulating because it can be resolved quickly. This effect brings a saving of 8 working hours a week. The Lean step in the medical record unit also has an effect on the inpatient unit. The redesign of the layout, better marking of files, and reduction of personnel distance with the printer, as well as the provision of space for patients, allow the nurses to move efficiently in the medical record room. This acceleration generates a reduction in patient walking distance of up to 30% and a reduction of 4% in treatment cancellation.

This step can be more efficient if the standard form is planned carefully so that it covers the entire value required by the patients. This matter can be achieved by mapping the patient value. With the value map, it can be seen where the patients move, beginning from admission to the hospital. These units have the information needed from the patient and provided by the medical record unit. If the unit cannot provide the required information, then the patient has to provide new information, which will therefore lower patient satisfaction. Of course, not all the information must be provided by the patients if the medical records cannot provide it. Most of the information will come from the previous procedure from the steps taken before. This procedure adds value, so it cannot be eliminated. Conversely, the procedure of asking the medical records unit or the patient about information that does not come from the previous step would not add value. This information should be collected in the first step, when the patients register. In other words, all the information is collected in one contact. This step may add another question for the patients to answer, but it will guarantee the patients that they no longer have to provide information when they are in the care system, and it also guarantees that the unit does not have to go back and forth in taking, filling out, and submitting information about the patients to other units. This step is applied in the research by Nasiri and able to be applied to 75% of the patients.[2]

The researchers have conducted studies on the Lean implementation of Kemang Medical Care, Jakarta, Indonesia, one of them on the medical record unit.[3] Steps are carried out by the Lean team, among others:

5S

5S is "a system to reduce waste and optimize productivity through regular workspace maintenance and use visual instructions to obtain more consistent operational results".[4] The original term actually comes from Japanese terms: *Seiri* (sorting), *Seiton* (Order), *Seiso* (cleanliness), *Seiketsu* (standardize), and *Shitsuke* (discipline).[5]

5S is used in this study as an indicator for dealing with preparation for work. The good and tidy workplace is prerequisite for the work implementation. Most can argue that neatness can inhibit creativity.[6] However, work in a hospital demands more in terms of conventionality, ethics, and health, which correlates with the clean place.[6] 5S has potential in mixing the layout and administration aspects. Even so, with careful guidance, the issues between arrangement of goods layout and administrative layout can be distinguished.

The Lean implementation process begins with doing the 5S program. All Lean team members sort the necessary and unnecessary equipment. Sorting is also done on the furniture, such as cabinets, desks, chairs, filing cabinets, whiteboards, and others. After the sorting process, the floor, walls, and corners of the room that are usually used to store unnecessary items need to be cleaned. Therefore, the workspace only contains the necessary equipment and furniture. Likewise with the drugs and medical devices; they are stored according to what is needed only. The result is the workspace becomes broader, more organized, and cleaner.

After the simplify step is completed, the unnecessary items (garbage) are sorted again to be stored in warehouses or disposed of by using red tag form. Warehousing follows the good and right rules of storage of goods. Red tag form is very helpful if in the future the goods are no longer needed. Standardization also includes the number and layout. The self-discipline step aims at monitoring and follow-up. In this case, the team leader will conduct inspections/audits, mainly regarding the cleanliness. Cleanliness of all goods is examined, both movable and immovable goods. Similarly, the floor and the walls are checked for cleanliness. Follow-up from the inspection is the instruction regarding cleaning which includes: activities undertaken, where it should be done, who does it, and when it should be done. The final step of 5S implementation is to provide a score for each unit. These scores are attached to a wall that is easily visible. Scores are held every month and done by the fellow team members in the cross unit.

Visual Management

Visual management is intended to determine, using Lean, the errors that occur in the healthcare service.[7] It happens because visual management allows the staff to look at the system at any time and find out whether or not there is a problem in the system.[8] The staff can immediately make improvement in the process that has a problem. Visual management can be implemented in *Seiton*[9] stage or executed after 5S.[10]

In our study, after implementing 5S, the next stage is to carry out the visual management. The intended visualization is meant is to make a sign, symbol, line, label, and coloring for easy retrieval, search, storage, and avoidance of mistakes. The examples of visualization are shown in Figure 12.1. The images show before and after Lean.

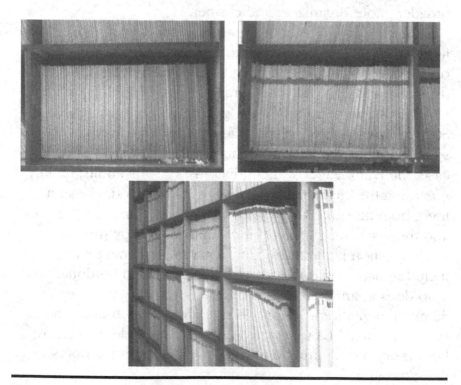

Figure 12.1   Visualization.

Kaizen

Literally, *kaizen* means change for the better.[11] These improvements are continual and apply the human appreciation principle.[12] Problems found, when viewed from the kaizen perspective, are actually a chance for improvement.[13] Kaizen can be seen as the final stage of Lean. It lifts the Lean from the operational point toward the epistemological point, where Lean is no longer separated but embedded in the heart of the organization. For this reason, kaizen becomes necessary to include in the study of Lean implementation in hospitals.

In our study in the medical record unit, the final stage of Lean is kaizen. Kaizen is done to create constant perfection and improvement. The form used is known as the A3 form. The form contains: reasons to make improvement, the current conditions and expected ideal conditions, the action/improvement steps toward the condition desired. Last, an indicator of the success of the improvement steps is carried out. More detail can be seen in Figure 12.2.

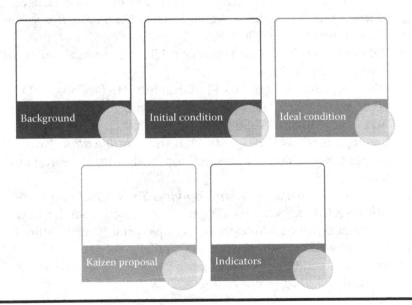

Figure 12.2   Lean project board/kaizen.

References

1. Fetterman, D.M. 2010. *Ethnography: Step-by-Step*. 3rd Edition. Los Angeles: Sage, p. 66.
2. Nasiri, S.D. 2009. *Lean Thinking and Queue Modelling in Healthcare*. Lancaster University Management School, p. 22. Retrieved from: http://www.leadingedgegroup.com/assets/uploads/Lean_Thinking_and_Queue_Modelling_in_Healthcare.pdf.
3. Iswanto, A.H. 2015. Adaptation of Lean Method Implementation as a Strategy to Improve the Organization Performance, Human Resources and Cost Efficiency of Hospital. Dissertation, University of Trisakti, Jakarta, Indonesia.
4. EPA. 2003. *Lean Manufacturing and Environment*. p. 10. [Online] Retrieved from: http://www.epa.gov/lean/performance/index.htm.
5. Viorel, B., Mihaela, C.A. 2009. Lean Hospital – Conceptualization and Instrumentation. *Ştiinţe Economice Tom*, XVIII: 78.
6. Vohs, K.D., Redden, J. P., Rahinel, R. 2013. Physical Order Produces Healthy Choices, Generosity, and Conventionality, Whereas Disorder Produces Creativity. *Psychological Science*, 24(9): 1860–1867.
7. de Koning, H., Verver, J.P. , van den Heuvel, J., Bisgaard, S., Does, R.J. 2006. Lean Six Sigma in Healthcare. *Journal for Healthcare Quality*, 28(2): 8.
8. Fillingham D. 2007. Can Lean Save Lives? *Leadership in Health Services* , 20(4): 231–241.
9. Hines S., Luna, K., Lofthus J., Marquardt, M., Stelmokas, D. 2008. Becoming a High Reliability Organization: Operational Advice for Hospital Leaders. (Prepared by the Lewin Group under Contract No. 290-04-0011.) *AHRQ Publication* No. 08-0022. Rockville, MD: Agency for Healthcare Research and Quality, p. 51.
10. ITC. 2004. *Principles of Lean Thinking: Tools & Techniques for Advanced Manufacturing*. ITC, p. 17. Retrieved from: http://www.itc.mb.ca/downloads/resources_by_topic/princ_lean%20thinking/PrinciplesofLeanThinkingRevD2004.pdf.
11. Emiliani, B. 2006. Origins of Lean Management in America. *Journal of Management History*, 12(2), 167–184.

12. Halling, B., Renstrom, J. 2011. *Lean and the Implementation Process – Managers Perspective on Change.* Paper presented at the "Arbetsliv i förändring" (FALF2011) Congress in Luleå, June 2011, p. 3.
13. MacDuffie, J.P. 1995. Human Resource Bundles and Manufacturing Performance: Organizational Logic and Flexible Production Systems in the World Auto Industry. *Industrial and Labor Relations Review*, 48(2): 197–221.

Chapter 13

Lean Implementation in the Hospital Facilities and Infrastructure Maintenance Units

Hospital Facilities and Infrastructure Maintenance Unit Issues

Hospital facilities and infrastructure maintenance units (further abbreviated as F&I) are units that are responsible for maintenance management. This unit is always in a dilemma between the effort to manage maintenance funds and give maximum maintenance. Maximum maintenance effort often needs much cash. The work volume for a unit can be big. For instance, for long-term facilities maintenance, there are 40 tasks that should be done regularly, from elevators to boiler procedures.[1] Meanwhile, the budget is wherever possible pressed so the F&I unit often works below optimum. This depends on whether the top leadership considers the F&I unit important or not. In addition, other units, both medical and nonmedical, depend on the F&I unit. Damage or unapproved equipment can endanger patients in many ways. Therefore, coordination problems can create serious impact in both party performances.

Bad coordination can be characterized by conflict between the F&I unit and others which are operational. Each party can blame the other. Damage can be blamed on the operational area for not being smart and not being careful, while the operational party can blame the F&I unit for not conducting checks on troubled facilities of infrastructure.

In certain schema, the F&I unit can be seen as an elite unit. In a Total Productive Maintenance (TPM) unit, maintenance responsibility is moved from F&I unit to officer. The F&I unit is only for management and only acts as a helper for employees in installing, upgrading, matching, and moving equipment, as well as becoming facilitator, supervisor, and trainer.[2] Generally, this scheme is implemented in a company with automatic production, like a cigarette factory or an airline, because the run of production depends on equipment, not on humans, and the hospital does not include them in company like them.

Generally, the maintenance unit in a hospital, especially in the housekeeping area, are seen as secondary employees because they do not have a health specialty. This is not actually true because they are also responsible for infection treatment. Dirty hospitals will cause infection to occur and decrease hospital health quality. In other words, housekeeping employees are those who have a health paradigm; it is different from doctors and nurses, who have a disease paradigm.

In Indonesia, the problems in the F&I unit are more severe. Many hospitals have staff that have inadequate qualification. In many cases, F&I officers are even outsourced. Hospitals would rather buy new equipment than maintain available equipment. Therefore, many F&I officers are used for housekeeping issues and few are allocated for technical problems. The budget for maintenance is unclear and minimized wherever possible. This more or less decreases the F&I unit image, as well as causing dissipation in term of finance, which in turn gives patients a burden.[3]

The F&I unit also experiences a dilemma between priority and work volume. In some way, if the work volume is small, then F&I workers will be pleased if there is a problem, although the problem is not significant. On the contrary, if the work volume is big, small problems which can actually be handled by a health officer will distract work; the maintenance officer is more pleased if they are given complex problems that need higher knowledge.

Lean Case Studies in Hospital Maintenance Units

Lean implementation which is run in an F&I unit can be seen from the example of the Red Cross Hospital in Beverwijk, the Netherlands.[4] In this hospital, there is a problem with facilities and infrastructure. Hospital officers input data to computers, which then produce blue coupons. These coupons contain the problem description and are submitted to maintenance officers. The officers then perform diagnosis and solve the problem. If the problem is solved, the officer reports it and the data are erased.

The problem of this scheme takes the longest time to be solved. In addition, problem accumulation happens due to active blue coupons becoming frequent. The Lean team soon find the solution to this problem. The root of the problem which is found is the unavailability of a standard work procedure for the F&I unit. In addition, arising problems are solved without considering the urgency or priority. Solutions published by the Lean team are:

1. Performing prevention steps. For instance, lights are turned off in the evening. This sustains the lightbulbs' life so they cannot be easily damaged.
2. Developing standard operational procedure which gives guidelines in facing damage and failure.
3. Arranging a work planning system where problems are divided based on the level of urgency.

4. Performance supervision and visual management in the form of rules to improve standard malfunction; this is then institutionalized and supervised.

Soon after it is implemented, the number of blue coupons decreases drastically. This reduction is said to save hospital budgets up to €200,000.

Another case of a hospital unit in University Hospital of University Health System, San Antonio, Texas, can be referred to.[5] Betty Smith, a new manager in the housekeeping unit, wonders why the employees never make suggestions for their work improvement, even though Smith asks them in every meeting. One of her employees, Sally, finally admits that she does not make suggestions for improvement because she does not have formal education and thus does not want to look stupid by making suggestions. The manager soon makes a three-month training program for her employees to increase their ability to recognize problems and to increase their confidence. After one and a half months, eventually, there is one person raising their hand to provide a suggestion in a meeting. The suggestion is provided by Sally. Sally says that she notices that a doctor complains to the emergency manager because the patient is delayed in the transfer from emergency to nursing room. According to Sally, this is partly caused by bedrooms not being cleaned soon after a patient is discharged. This happens, in turn, because thee nurse secretary does not give an estimate to the housekeeping unit of when patients will be discharged. The unit is informed only when the patients have been discharged or after the emergency unit asks nurses to provide room for a patient. As a result, there is a delay of more than one hour for the time required for housekeeping officers to respond. When the housekeeping manager meets the head of nursing, the head of nursing reports that the time required is three hours.

A Lean team is soon formed which consists of the manager of nursing, nurses, housekeeping staff, including Sally, nurse supervisor, and unit secretary. The duty of this team is discussing problems and finding solutions. Solutions produced are:

1. The nurse supervisor sends an e-mail containing the patient discharge plan from certain rooms the day before to housekeeping before midnight. Housekeeping officers who work in the evening will receive the e-mail and post it to housekeeping. Morning-shift housekeeping officers plan daily activity to be in line with the input of the list.
2. Two baskets are kept in nursing, one to mark clean rooms and one to mark dirty rooms.
3. When patients are discharged from the room, a nurse will put red paper on the bed to mark that the room is dirty.
4. The housekeeping officer cleans the room. When the room has been cleaned and is ready to welcome the patient, the red paper from the "dirty" basket is taken and green paper with the same room number is placed on the "clean" basket.
5. The nurse looks at the clean basket to know which rooms which are empty and clean so when the emergency unit wants to transfer patients, nurses only need to direct the patient to the room.

The result of this Lean implementation is surprising for all parties. The head of nursing extends gratitude due to room exchange decreasing drastically from three hours and more to 30 minutes. In the next housekeeping meeting, the manager extends gratitude toward Sally and all people who participate. Their ideas have increased patient, nurse, and doctor satisfaction. When the meeting is done, three people raise their hands and give new problems to be solved and suggestions of how to solve them.

From the aforementioned examples, we can see that problems in the housekeeping unit are more or less the same in Indonesia and in developed countries. They tend to be either paid less attention or lack confidence in cooperation aspects among units and communication among units, likewise in interaction between unit and planning department.[6]

In the study we conduct in the housekeeping unit, the same thing also happens. Improvement of Lean implementation only increases by 1% of the full-time equivalent (FTE) indicator in three months of implementation, although in six months implementation, the indicator increases by 12% after the sixth month into baseline.[7]

The incident of very low average change on housekeeping FTE for three months since the implementation shows the low ability of the housekeeping sector to adapt to Lean implementation. The cause of the low housekeeping ability relates to the nature of its management, which is way general. The responsibilities of this area involve cleanliness, security, vehicles, equipment, laundry, goods inventory, and storage. The area of responsibility involves the kitchen, patients' rooms, waiting room, laundry, and so on. The general character cause Lean implementation effect should delay for a long time for preparation. In addition, the big workload with little incentive compared to other areas of the hospital can contribute to the difficulty of Lean implementation, which affects housekeeping FTE.

There are three other explanations for the low of Lean effect on housekeeping FTE. Critics of Lean state that Lean is implemented badly by not considering the human aspect from Lean philosophy.[8] This result makes Lean seem like a new producing machine which only gives profits to capital owners, not to the workers. Although our study is conducted in the context of health workers who have a strong ethical foundation compared to manufacturers, the housekeeping unit includes an area that does not have strong ethical ties. Therefore, the perception in the housekeeping worker area that they actually obtain work instruction which incriminates them can occur only because of the new name, which is Lean. The general reaction can only work well when supervising is performed; when there is no supervising, things return to the initial condition.

The third possibility is the lack of appreciation for the work of other professionals. The housekeeping area is an incentives area emotionally. In a hospital, customers are patients, and they come to find not cleanliness but recovery. Patients recover because of doctors', pharmacists', and their assistants' service, not by the service by housekeeping officers. Therefore, housekeeping officers do not obtain satisfaction from their job. Even if they are paid with low incentives, if there is appreciation for their work, they can feel proud, like in gardening work. However, they tend to not be considered in work at hospitals. In other words, housekeeping officers' work is seen as secondary work in hospitals, including the outpatient unit.

The condition of the housekeeping officers is regrettable. The study indicates that experience of unfairness in organizations can make people angry and stressed, which, in turn, can cause excessive worries, depression, low work satisfaction, insomnia, and heart disease.[9] As a reaction, health officers or housekeeping officers can produce counterproductive work behavior like organizational deviation, aggression in the workplace, or anti-social behavior,[10] especially if the officer has low self-control.[11] A housekeeping officer can assume that the mistake he makes is actually the responsibility of hospital, not him.[12] On the other side, if employees are not treated fairly, then the justice will affect the third party, which relates to the party that obtains fairness. For instance, if a manager is fair to housekeeping officers, then housekeeping officers will also be fair to the customers.[11] In addition, officers will perform organizational citizenry by assisting other employees in finishing their jobs.[11]

Bad perception toward housekeeping can be observed by comparing them with physician assistant or pharmacist assistant jobs. When a physician assistant or pharmacist assistant has good performance, they are appreciated, while the same thing may not occur to a housekeeping officer. On the contrary, patients can easily complain when there is bad service from a housekeeping officer, like the spread of garbage and inappropriate attitude of cleaning officers. This is also indicated by patients or visitors who do not greet the cleaning officers. Likewise, jobs like cleaning, which is part of housekeeping, intrinsically drive bad mentality. This is indicated when a cleaning officer has to clean a room or floor and then a patient or other professional mess it up so it as though their job only has a short-term effect. With this condition, then, mentally, housekeeping officers do not have a strong motivation to work better. This is then manifested in lack of work spirit, negative face expression, and sentimental behavior when their works are not appreciated.

The fourth explanation of the finding of housekeeping FTE is the low educational background of the officers in this sector. Generally, housekeeping work is a job that does not require an education, so everyone can do it. Indonesian Governmental Regulation No. 32 of 1996 on Healthcare Professionals, for instance, does not include cleaning service workers as part of healthcare professionals. This is affecting the view that housekeeping work is the last alternative, filled by people who are not included with the other professionals, brimming with knowledge, who work in the hospital. In some hospitals, especially governmental/public hospitals, housekeeping professionals, even in outsourcing, can bring stress. With low educational background, the level of understanding of professionalism or instruction, as well as special terms, can be lower to than that of other professions; thus, Lean implementation is hampered.

This implies that attention needs to be given to the housekeeping unit. In future Lean implementation, intervention should address the housekeeping area as well so that the Lean effect can be maximal. This intervention involves more focused incentives and training.

References

1. Tweedy, J.T. 2005. *Healthcare Hazard Control and Safety Management.* 2nd Edition. Boca Raton, FL: CRC Press.
2. Schonberger, R. 2008. *Best Practices in Lean Six Sigma Process Improvement: A Deeper Look.* Hoboken, NJ: John Wiley & Sons.

3. Rokx, C., Schieber, G., Harimurti, P., Tandon, A., Somanathan, A. 2009. *Health Financing in Indonesia: A Reform Road Map*. World Bank.
4. De Koning, H., Verver, J.P.S., van den Heuvel, J., Bisgaard, S., Does, R.J.M. 2006. Lean Six Sigma in Healthcare. *Journal for Healthcare Quality*, 28(2): 4–11.
5. Pickens, J.. 2005. Attitudes and Perceptions. In *Organizational Behaviour in Health Care*. ed. N. Borkowski. Sudbury, MA: Jones and Bartlett Publishers, pp. 43–76.
6. Clay, J.M., Palakurthi, R. 2003. Employee Satisfaction: Impact on Organizational Success, 2003. *Annual International CHRIE Conference and Exposition Proceedings*, pp. 100–104.
7. Iswanto, A.H. 2015. Adaptation of Lean Method Implementation as a Strategy to Improve the Organization Performance, Human Resources and Cost Efficiency of Hospital. Dissertation, University of Trisakti, Jakarta, Indonesia.
8. Graban, M. 2010. Notes from Dr. Brent James at the Shingo Prize, Part 2 – Comments on Lean. Retrieved from: http://www.leanblog.org/2010/06/notes-from-dr-brent-james-at-the-shingo-prize-part-2/.
9. Masterson, S.S., Lewis, K., Goldman, B.M., Taylor, M.S. 2000. Integrating Justice and Social Exchange: The Differing Effects of Fair Procedures and Treatment on Work Relationships. *Academy of Management Journal*, 43: 738–748.
10. Kivimaki, M., Ferrie, J.E., Brunner, E., Head, J., Shipley, M.J., Vahtera, J., Marmot, M.G. 2005. Justice at Work and Reduced Risk of Coronary Heart Disease among Employees: The Whitehall II Study. *Archives of Internal Medicine*, 165: 2245–2251.
11. Barger, P.B. 2009. *Service Without a Smile?! Exploring the Roles of Customer Injustice, Anger and Individual Differences in Emotional Deviance*. PhD dissertation, Bowling Green State University, p. 6.
12. Greenberg, J. 1990. Employee Theft as a Reaction to Underpayment Inequity: The Hidden Cost of Pay Cuts. *Journal of Applied Psychology*, 75: 561–568.

Chapter 14

Lean Implementation in the Referral Unit

Referral Unit Issues

The referral unit deals with transfer problems from other hospitals or from community health centers and clinics. The advancement of this unit highly relies on information technology related to clinical information among hospitals, or between hospitals and community health centers or clinics. If good coordination is available, then patients' quality and safety will be assured; also, patients will have a positive experience related to the nursing transition. Therefore, nursing coordination is the key development for the referral unit.

Much dissipation occurs when miscommunication and discontinuity occur in nursing transition. This dissipation can be in the form of dangerous medical and nursing errors and unnecessary repeated referral. In addition, this may increase cost due to repeated tests and procedures.

A general step that is taken is cooperating with other health service providers. In New York state, the government has provided regional data exchange which potentially increases patients' information exchange on nursing points, so it eliminates many errors and duplications.[1]

In the health system in Indonesia, the referral system follows the flow, which is clear hierarchically. The village delivery house and the village health center refer to the community health center and the auxiliary health center; the community health center and the auxiliary health center refer to district hospital; district hospital refers to provincial hospital; and provincial hospital refers to central/general hospital. However, this has not removed the competition between private hospitals and clinics. A hospital which does not have expected quality and structures by certain parties will lack income because of untrustworthiness. Therefore, every hospital should develop a clear referral guide, as well as compete to increase the quality, so it can be trusted by other health service providers to refer their patients there. If the hospital has had a good reputation through Lean implementation, then it possibly becomes a referral for other hospitals to send patients to.

Referral for patients may be in the form of patients who come from another place to the hospital or patients who are referred to another place by the hospital.

Patients Who Are Referred from Another Place

In this case, usually, the hospital or health center that conduct the referral are aware of anything required and enclose it with the patient; or else, they first call the hospital that the patient will be referred to in order to confirm the data they need.

A study conducted by Rosmulder on referred patients in the emergency unit of Academic Medical Center, Amsterdam can serve as an example.[2] Like the emergency unit in any place, the main problem in this unit is the waiting time. The waiting time in the emergency unit can threaten the patient and, in some cases, also threaten the officer due to the anger of the patient and their companion. Waiting time rises due to patient fluctuation, which is very unpredictable. If only the patient's arrival could be predicted, nurses would not need to wait for patients in their spare time and patients also would not need to wait for nurses during rush hours.[3]

Some emergency patients are actually predictable, and these patients are referral-type patients.[2] In the Rosmulder case, 20% of emergency patients are referral patients. Referral patients generally need 24 hours to arrive but seldom come soon[2], although usually they have more serious illnesses than non-referred patients.[2] In addition, referred patients spend three hours in the emergency unit on average, twice as long than non-referred patients.[2]

The procedure performed by the doctor who refers first consults the specialist in the hospital. The specialist then informs the nurse to prepare for patient's arrival. When the patient arrives, the nurse directly performs a diagnostic examination. The procedure offered by Rosmulder is when the doctor calls the specialist, the specialist directs the doctor to nurse. The nurse then discusses the arrival time with the doctor, who makes the referral based on the patient's condition and situation in the emergency unit.[2] Unfortunately, this plan fails to be implemented, although it is supported by the management of the emergency unit. The specialist argues that "emergency patients cannot wait," "the doctor who makes the referral cannot examine whether or not the patient can wait," and "this is an additional job for the specialist." The root of problem is actually caused by the fact that the specialist who receives the referral does not work in the emergency unit and, therefore, does not have an instruction structure which is bound to the emergency unit management.[2] In addition, the parties involved have not prepared for any change. They are not sure that the new procedure brings any advantages while the old procedure has worked well for many years and become the status quo.[4]

The idea of Rosmulder is actually good because it shows the referral unit's role in eliminating waiting time in the emergency unit. The problem lies in Lean implementation preparation that is less mature in one way or another; the nature of various information is bad among the health practitioners who are studied. Information of referred patients is worthy information. The ability to exchange, build, integrate, and use it among hospitals determines the quality of health service provided to the patient. Information technology will be a big help because it provides fast response, patient service, and data division.[5] This is way better if it is supported with accuracy, adequacy, haste, and credibility of patients' data information.[6] However, information technology is only an infrastructure, and without wise users, the result will not be optimum. For better results of Lean implementation, the steps from the previous chapters can be adopted in eight steps, which involve: (1) audit, (2) problem identification, (3) finding solution, (4) gaining acceptance, (5) planning, (6) implementing, (7) controlling, and (8) return to audit.

A positive case can be seen from the Sunshine Coast Health Service, Queensland, Australia, case.[7] One of the Lean implementation purposes is simplifying the referral process in the outpatient unit. In the first step, all parties are involved in the planning phase, starting from medical staff, nurses, and employees from all sectors. Lean steps which can be implemented involve: Learn to See, value flow mapping, eliminate, combine, reduce, simplify (ECRS) cycle, and plan, do, study, act (PDSA) cycle. The result of this Lean intervention is a decrease in the waiting time from referral to face-to-face contact from 81.3 days into 31 days, an increase in the number of referrals accepted per month from 6.75 into 30.5, and the number of referrals seen per month reaches 15.62. The decrease continues to occur for family waiting time from referral to the initial meeting. In addition, the number of referrals which are rejected decreases from 23% to only 0.8% or only 2 people of 246 referrals in six months of implementation.

The same thing occurred in Caboolture Hospital in Queensland, Australia, which decreased patient waiting time in the outpatient unit, which also caused an increase in the number of referrals by more than 88 people in a year.[8] The strategy is to classify some referred patients to the fast clinic.

A referred patient in this category is a patient who in the review of information enclosed to him or her can be handled in one meeting and in a shorter amount of time, as well as the possibility of there being only one meeting required.

Patients Who Are Referred to Another Place

In a case where a hospital should refer a patient to another place, the factor that needs to be considered is treatment transition for the patient. When this happens, the hospital should have a risk evaluation and nursing evaluation device. With this device, hospitals can provide a well-documented referral plan containing anything which has been tested and diagnosed, as well as risks that can be experienced by patients.[9] If the referral is performed because patient got well and therefore the referral is brought to a clinic or a community health center, hospitals should do follow-up nursing ten days after release. For patients over 80 years old, follow-up nursing should be performed a day after release.

The nursing transition strategy performed by Mercy Medical Center, Cedar Rapids, Iowa, can serve as an example.[10] An interdisciplinary meeting is conducted every day regarding patients' release potential, patients' release plan, and related questions. In meeting rooms, boards containing lists of patients that will be home or referred are provided. In addition, boards containing data regarding nurses' names, release-related issues, date of meeting that can be attended by patient family members, release date prediction, the purpose of the patient that day, and medical procedures or tests that will be performed next. At the bedside, there are report files which are filled by nurses detailing who is in and out, update in time of shift exchange, which is witnessed and consulted together with the patient wherever possible.

Nurses are responsible for preparing comprehensive release plans involving food, activity, nursing in the home (if not referred), medicine consumption, follow-up nursing schedule, teaching the patient regarding their release, follow-up nursing, and what should they do after release. This process is created in a very standardized way so that doctors and nurses do not forget their duty. Nurses are also responsible for making the medical instructions for the nurses or doctors who become the referral. This instruction will be submitted to the party who is referred when the patient is released.

If the patient is released, not referred, and if the hospital has a big enough budget, the patient can be equipped with a long-distance electronic monitoring device. This device can monitor the patient's vital signs and send the data daily to the hospital. When the hospital notices that the symptom is getting worse, the hospital will call the patient. The follow-up step can be in the form of a call to the doctor, an increase in dose, a hospital visit, or going directly to the emergency unit. Another way of monitoring is by calling the patient periodically through phone or even periodical house visits. If the patient is referred to a special nursing house, the hospital does not release its responsibility but together with the facility ensures the patient's necessities are satisfied.

The steps implemented by Mercy Medical Center resulted in a prehospitalization decrease of 47%, a cost reduction of $600,000 in two years, and nursing appropriateness increase from 70.8% to 91.8% in four years. This case is an example of how a post-release nursing transition program can give good results to patients and reduce costs for the hospital. The same case is also found in the University of Colorado Health Science Center, Denver, Colorado, which finds that transitional nursing decreases patients' possibility of experiencing rehospitalization for the same illness or condition.[11]

References

1. Burke, G. 2012. Trends and Changes in New York State Health Care System: Implications for the Certificate of Need (CON) Process. United Hospital Fund, 13.

2. Rosmulder, R.W. 2011. *Improving Healthcare Delivery with Lean Thinking: Action Research in an Emergency Department.* PhD dissertation, Universiteit Twente, 3.

3. Hopp W., Spearman M. (2000). *Factory Physics.* 2nd Edition. Singapore: McGraw-Hill.

4. Ham C. 2003. Improving the Performance of Health Services: The Role of Clinical Leadership. *The Lancet,* 361: 1978–1980.

5. Jayaraj, A., Sethi, V. 2010. Information Systems Infrastructures for Supply Chain Visibility. *Proceedings of the Southern Association for Information Systems Conference,* Atlanta, GA, March. 77.

6. Li, S., Ragu-Nathan, B., Ragu-Nathan, T.S., Rao, S.S. 2006. The Impact of Supply Chain Management Practices on Competitive Advantage and Organizational Performance. *Omega,* 34: 107–124, hal. 110; see also Feldmann M., Müller S. 2003. An Incentive Scheme for True Information Providing in Supply Chains. *Omega,* 31(2): 63–73; Monczka, R.M., Petersen, K.J., Handfield, R.B., Ragatz, G.L. 1998. Success Factors in Strategic Supplier Alliances: The Buying Company Perspective. *Decision Science,* 29(3): 5553–5577; Holmberg, S. 2000. A Systems Perspective on Supply Chain Measurements. *International Journal of Physical Distribution and Logistics Management,* 30(10): 847–868; Lee, H.L, Padmanabhan, V., Whang, S. 1997. Information Distortion in a Supplychain: The Bullwhip Effect. *Management Science,* 43(4): 546–558; McAdam, R., McCormack, D. 2001. Integrating Business Processes for Global Alignment and Supplychain Management. *Business Process Management Journal,* 7(2): 113–130.

7. Saxon, R., Trevor, C. 2011. Pediatric Models of Care – Outpatient Service Delivery. *14th Annual ACHS Quality Improvement Awards,* pp. 26–29.

8. Diplock, R., Kilah, M., Woolfield, N. 2011. Improving Waiting Times for Category Two Patients in the Pediatric Outpatient Department. *14th Annual ACHS Quality Improvement Awards,* pp. 50–51.

9. Hughes, R.G. 2009. Tools and Strategies for Quality Improvement and Patient Safety. In *Patient Safety and Quality: An Evidence-Based Handbook for Nurses.* Rockville, MD: Agency for Healthcare Research and Quality, p. 29.

10. Silow-Carrol, S., Lashbrook, A. 2011. Mercy Medical Center: Reducing Readmissions through Clinical Excellence, Palliative Care, and Collaboration. *The Commonwealth Fund Case Study Report,* March

11. Shih, A., Davis, K., Schoenbaum, S.C., Gauthier, A., Nuzum, R., McCarthy, D. 2008. Organizing the US Health Care Delivery System for High Performance, *The Commonwealth Fund Report*, 6; see also Naylor, M.D. 2006. Transitional Care: A Critical Dimension of the Home Healthcare Quality Agenda. *Journal of Healthcare Quality*, 28(1): 48–54 and Davis, K. *A Patient-Centered Health System*. American Hospital Association Robert Larson Memorial Lecture, Washington, DC, May 2, 2006. Coleman, E.A., Smith, J.D., Frank, J.C., Min, S.J., Parry, C., Kramer, A.M. 2004. Preparing Patients and Caregivers to Participate in Care Delivered Across Settings: The Care Transitions Intervention. *Journal of the American Geriatrics Society*, 52: 1817–1825. Coleman, E.A. Windows of Opportunity for Improving Transitional Care. Presentation to *The Commonwealth Fund Commission on a High Performance Health System*, March 30, 2006.

Chapter 15

Lean Implementation in the Administration and Management Unit

Change Management in the Administration and Management Unit

Administration and management (AdM) are the main infra-structure of the hospital as an organization. The AdM unit is responsible for managing financial and overall hospital set-ting issues. When we think about Lean implementation in this unit, it is not only dealing with the implementation on one part only but on all parts of the hospital. Therefore, we can take the example of how the administration and management functions of the hospital run the Lean on the whole hospital.

In the context of Lean implementation, the most relevant management topic is change management. To perform the change management, hospitals must believe that change can be organized in a structure through a number of steps.[1] This will bring individuals, teams, and organizations from one old condition into the new condition desired.[2] Changes need to be regulated because they influenced by many external factors, and if the internal factors are not controlled, these external factors, in the end, will ruin what the hospital aspires to.[3]

Change management is associated with the various techniques used to bring a change in businesses, including hospitals.[4] The change could be a change in the process, structure, technology, staff, or culture.[5] In the Lean context, it means that the change is more to the process for short-term and culture for long-term.

Although it is directed at the process and cultural change, good change management will impact various aspects in the hospital. In total, there are seven hospital aspects which can be viewed as the entrance to change management. When the AdM unit try to make changes to a door, then the other doors should also adapt to these changes. This adaptation effort should be done regularly through the wise steps run by the AdM unit (Figure 15.1).

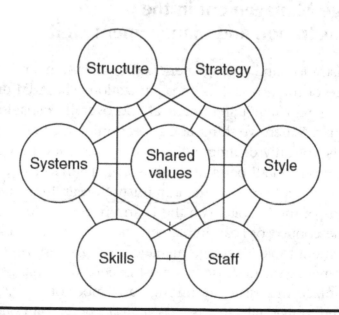

Figure 15.1   Seven entrances of change management. (From Payne, A. 2005. *Handbook of CRM: Achieving Excellence in Customer Management*. Amsterdam, the Netherlands: Elsevier, p. 348.)

The seven entrances are summarized as 7S, namely:

1. Structure: Structure changes are marked by changes on the organization map, which shows how and to whom tasks are divided and integrated.
2. Strategy: Strategy changes are marked by changes in the set of coherent actions to gain sustainable competitive advantage.
3. Style: Style changes show how managers behave in using time, attention, and symbolic actions. The style here is the management style, and it usually happens when the leadership changes, but it can also be that a manager changes his style for specific demands.
4. Staff: Staff changes are marked by changes in the hospital demographics, for example, the number of nurses, physicians, and so on. It is also important to note that staff changes are not personality changes from the same individual.
5. Skill: Skill changes are marked by changes in the organization's ability to handle issues or work. Usually, skills changes are accompanied by changes in technology. It is also important to note that the skill changes here do not mean changes in a person's ability, such as changes in competence.
6. System: Process and technology changes are included in the system changes. The bottom line is the change in how things are done from day to day.
7. Shared values: Cultural changes are included in the shared values change. These changes are characterized by what is right and wrong in the eyes of the hospital and most people working at the hospital.

From the 7S framework, when a hospital attempts to implement Lean in the short-term in terms of the system that Lean applies sustainably, the hospital needs to make changes in aspects such as shared values, skill, staff, style, strategy, and the structure of the hospital. These changes will be long-term and culminate in a hospital that fully adopts Lean inside, not only at every unit in the hospital but also in the infrastructure that sustains it.

Change always follows three stages. When the hospital discovers an issue and it demands to be solved through a change such as Lean implementation, then the hospital has entered a melting stage. When the implementation is done, this is when the changes enter the moving stage. If the implementation is successful, including the spread of all 7S dimensions, and the hospital changes the form, then the change has come to the freezing point.[7]

Typically, a change management step may be considered when Lean implementation is successful in one of the units in the hospital. When the hospital feels the effects of such implementation, the idea to spread the Lean implementation to all parts of the hospital emerges. When this decision is made, change management steps must be followed because Lean handling for one hospital will be much more complex than just in one unit, which tend to be homogeneous. AdM must plan carefully, implement organization, and control the ongoing changes.[8]

Planning made by AdM should include a variety of the following success factors to ensure the success of change management in the Lean hospital. These considerations include, among others:[9]

1. Strong leadership: Due to the fact that the changes that will be run will include many units and various aspects of hospital organization, authoritative leadership that can implement these changes well is needed.
2. Respected clinic champions: Although all the employees will be involved, there will be a structure and it requires a leader. In this structure, the physician, nurse, and other staff member that is appreciated by most employees must be chosen carefully, so it is able to ease the accepted

change. Each group, as well as each unit, must have a representative. Each of them later does not work alone but in an integrated team. This is necessary because the changes, in the end, will culminate in individual change. Change management speaks at the organizational level, but it will be associated also at the individual level, especially individual emotion.[10] Many individuals will resist change not because the change is right but because it is not fun. Emotions are contagious. You can see how a debate would end up in chaos if one party is unable to control his emotions. Therefore, AdM should consider the individual emotion issue when making changes in all organization dimensions and ensure it is done through individuals who have the charisma to bring positive emotions to other people.

3. Full confidence communication: When we talk about changes on the emotional side, then it will soon be associated with power relations or organizational politics.[11] Negative emotions often appear when someone is injured politically, for example, in issues related to command, authority, wages, injustice, powerlessness, and so on. This issue can be seen, for example, in how the marketing department fights with the design section in a technology company. There is no need to even go so far; quarrels between the medical records section and other sections in the hospital also commonly happen. The hospital is an organization that has good structure; this structure looks dead, in the sense that it does not consider the feelings of the people involved in it. AdM personnel cannot simply give orders to other units to change, even though in the organizational sense he has right to do it. An order must be accompanied by an understanding, and this why it is important that the Lean concept is understood by every worker in the hospital. Lean is not to add their workload, not to make them dizzy, but rather to make their work easier and more appreciated. This understanding should

be given to everyone, even those who are not directly involved. AdM can invite other people to understand, commit, and feel ownership for the change that they will do together.

4. The right attitude when faced with an obstacle from the individual side: This attitude feels a bit cruel since it is basically saying "participating or out." Anyone who hinders change must be listened to, have the change described to them, and made to understand. If they still refuse, it means the problem is not the change itself but in other aspects that they do not want to tell. If they do not want to tell, it will be better if they do not hinder change. If left unchecked, they will transmit the negative emotions and destroy the newly built structure. Nevertheless, this expulsion step must be done strategically through a joint session of what are the right steps to remove the barriers so that every project member has the responsibility for the decision.

5. Willingness to take risks: AdM needs to ask for a statement that every member is willing to take risks. Things that need to be considered are whether the changes have to be done, what challenges may be encountered in the future, and how the obstacles can be eliminated.

6. A systematic and comprehensive approach: Here, all 7S aspects that have been formulated previously are brought. In addition to 7S (staff, skill, system, shared values, style, strategy, and structure), compensation issues such as the payroll, awards, and bonus system need to be planned.

7. In-depth employee involvement: All employees of the hospital should be involved in the change without exception. It is easy because there is a new structure that is ready to mobilize the human resources in each unit in the hospital.

8. Permanent employee empowerment: Empowerment here means to delegate to the project team the authority to make decisions. It would be very contrary to the Lean principles if the team in the end also has to coordinate

and request a decision from above through a long bureaucratic process.

9. Changes perceived as belonging to the majority of employees: The employees can feel at home if they are the one who plans and executes the change. Therefore, as far as possible, all employees are involved in the decision-making process and in the implementation of decisions.

10. The existence of financial resources: The issue of money is a sensitive issue, and, therefore, discussing it is sometimes neglected or performed in reverse, namely, the work is done first and then the wage is given. This is wrong if you want to make changes. The financial resources have to be allocated in advance, as well as incentives to foster change. If the employee works more than expected, incentives in the form of bonuses can be added last.

11. The existence of education and training at all levels: Lean implementation requires an understanding of what Lean and any associated techniques are, not only cognitively but also empirically. This means that there is a future for a particular representation, and, if possible, all employees go through training and education of Lean implementation, guided by the experienced mentors. If possible, use specialized practitioners who provide consulting services of Lean implementation issues.

12. Commitment to see the changes through to the end: Overall changes are difficult to understand if we only look in a hurry on certain aspects. The initial stage of change can instead give negative results because the hospital is still learning by way of trial and error or because a lot of parts are still trying to adapt to the new environment. If in this initial stage the employee spirit has gone down, it also has bad impacts. Therefore, an understanding should be given and there should be efforts to build employee commitment to work until the final changes are seen. Changes take time, and time must be understood by all who work in change.

The following story may illustrate how a hospital makes changes on a whole.[12] Nyack Hospital in New York initially experiences a crisis at the emergency department. The crisis is, for example, characterized by the number of patients who have to wait up to eight hours for care, and approximately 3% of patients leave the emergency department without treatment.

In 2006, BD Lab, a Lean consultant agency, makes a presentation at Nyack Hospital. CEO David Freed then realizes the importance of Lean to eliminate all types of waste and immediately cooperates with the agency. Freed makes long-term plans to transform the hospital into a hospital that is appreciated by the communities and provides benefits. The first step is the implementation in the emergency department.

The Lean Steps

The Lean team immediately sets up eight working steps to resolve the problem in the emergency department. The eight steps include (1) audit, (2) identify problems, (3) find solutions, (4) gain acceptance, (5) plan, (6) implement, (7) control, and (8) back to audit. Details of these steps are as follows:

1. Audit: The Lean team and the hospital conduct an audit on emergency department work.
2. Identify problems: After training, observation, making of value stream map, and analysis, it is found that the problems encountered by the emergency department are caused by:
   a. Non-standard work processes and staff assignments that do not reflect the actual work activities.
   b. Physical layout that is not optimal, causing bad teamwork, ineffective communication, and delay of patient care.
   c. Poor communication between the bed control and the nursing unit, causing a delay in the placement of patients and generating the existence of temporary beds.

    d. Limited information technology in the number and placement, thus causing a delay in the registration and data search.

    e. Messed-up staff schedule because the patient volume is unpredictable and training is limited.

    f. Administrative work that is not centralized and documents that are not easily accessible.

    g. Supporting units such as laboratory and radiology are often late.

    h. Equipment and supplies stored in a location that is not convenient for the staff.

3. Find solutions: Solutions made, among others:

    a. Have a meeter-greeter protocol wherein any officer who meets with patients first must welcome them.

    b. Pair the triage of the bedside with registration at the bedside.

    c. Build a 30-minute service standard motto; this is a medical treatment process at the emergency department where the longest time is 30 minutes after patient arrival.

    d. Redesign the information system with more reliable information technology in dealing with order entry, full patient documentation, and calculating the cost of the patient.

    e. Redesign of the physical layout to make it more conducive for teamwork.

    f. Cross the training of nursing staff for flexibility of schedule and patient exchange.

    g. Fund the purchase of information technology devices such as printers, fax machines, etc. to add anything that is lacked.

    h. Develop a mobile registration basket and wireless technology to accelerate the registration and quick access to medical records.

    i. Give a guarantee of 30–90 minutes for lab testing and radiology services.

j. Enable trash to be quickly filled and thereby quickly emptied.

k. Purchase IV poles and additional ECGs.

4. Gain acceptance: In this step, the team and the hospital meet all units, describe the 30-minute service standards applied in the emergency department, and ask for cooperation from all units. In addition, the campaign is carried out by radio, newspapers, bus ads, and billboards. The compensation given to the patients if late is a letter of apology and a $25 voucher to spend at a supermarket.

5. Plan: Included in Steps 3 and 4.

6. Implement: Running Step 3.

7. Control: Supervise continuously, ask issues to the nurses, and instantly respond.

8. Audit: The results obtained include:

   a. The incoming patients process declines from 13 steps to seven steps.

   b. There is a decrease in patients who go unnoticed from 3% to 1.6% in two months, and in two years this is to be 0%. Continuous result with fluctuation only reaches 0.08%.

   The length of stay declines from 5 hours to less than 4 hours.

   c. The 30-minute service standard increases from 37% in the first month to 97% in the sixth month.

   d. Patient satisfaction increases from 17% to 91% in four years and reaches 99% in the third year.

   e. Total visits increase from 38,600 to 53,000 in three years.

   f. Revenue increases from $4 million loss into a profit of $4.8 million in three years.

Seeing the progress in the emergency department, AdM decides to implement it in all units at the hospital. Positive results are also found in implementations in other units. It includes a decline of lab results delay from 5% to below 1% without adding the staff; radiology turnaround time (TAT) declines to less than one hour; and there is a decline in transportation time. These steps are followed by a certification step where some staff members are trained to represent all parts of the hospital to achieve the expertise level in Lean. The certification process is shown based on the achievements in reducing waste in the section which they represent in the hospital. On average, staff earn a certificate as a Lean leader after six months. After the contract with the Lean consultants, staff who have got the certificate will continue their work in maintaining hospital sustainability.

Now, Lean has become an indispensable part of Nyack Hospital. It makes it easier to implement change. The employees feel happy when asked about what is good and what is problematic and feel excited to provide solutions for the advancement of the hospital.

References

1. Hallencreutz, J. 2009. *Models and Meaning: On Management Models and Systems of Meaning When Implementing Change.* Master's thesis, Lulea University of Technology, p. 13.
2. Burnes, B. 2009. *Managing Change.* Upper Saddles River, NJ: Prentice Hall; Dawson, P. 2003. *Understanding Organizational Change.* London, UK: Sage; Kotter, J.P. 1996. *Leading Change.* Boston, MA: Harvard Business School Press.
3. Todnem, R. 2005. Organizational Change Management: A Critical Review. *Journal of Change Management*, 5(4): 369–380.
4. Laudon, K.C., Laudon, J.P. 2009. *Essentials of Management Information Systems.* 8th Edition. New York: Pearson, p. 20.
5. Combe, C. 2006. *Introduction to e-Business: Management and Strategy.* Amsterdam, the Netherlands: Elsevier, p.256.
6. Payne, A. 2005. *Handbook of CRM: Achieving Excellence in Customer Management.* Amsterdam, the Netherlands: Elsevier, p. 348.
7. Meliala, A., Hill, P. 2009. Introduction: Organization and Individual Change: Managing for Change. In Utarini, A., Schmidt-Ehry, G., Hill, P. (eds.) *Hospital Management Training: New Ways to Improve Services in Indonesia.* Jakarta,

Indonesia: GTZ, p. 72; see also Burns, B. 2004. Kurt Lewin and Complexity Theories: Back to the Future? *Journal of Change Management*, 4(4): 309–325; and Lewin, K. 1946. *Resolving Social Conflicts*. New York, NY: Harper.

8. Raschulte, T. 2007. *Understanding How to Change: An Inductive Determination of How Agents of State Government Plan, Lead, and Sustain Change*. PhD dissertation, Regent University, VA, p. 59.

9. InfoFinders. 2010. *Leading Practices in Emergency Department Patient Experience*. Ontario Hospital Association, p. 29.

10. Becker, K.L. 2008. Fostering Unlearning to Facilitate Change and Innovation. In *Academy of Management 2008 Annual Meeting Proceedings—The Questions We Ask*, 8–13 August 2008, Anaheim, CA, p. 24.

11. Pieterse, J.H., Caniëls, M.C.J., Homan, T. 2012. Professional Discourses and Resistance to Change. *Journal of Organizational Change Management*, 25(6): 798–818.

12. BD Laboratory Consulting Services. 2011. *Lean Journey Helps Transform Nyack Hospital, Improving Quality, Efficiency & Patient Satisfaction*. BD Lab White Paper.

Chapter 16

Conclusion

The Principles of Lean

Lean is the cultural commitment of organizations to implementing the scientific method in designing, conducting, and improving work sustainably through teamwork, bringing in better and measurable value to the patients and stakeholders of other hospitals.[1] It shortens the time between ordering and service delivery by eliminating waste from the service flow value.[2] Lean is associated not only with the technical aspects but also the social aspect.[3] Ultimately, Lean will provide advantages in financial terms for the organization.[4]

From the explanation described throughout this book, we have seen how Lean managed to improve the effectiveness and efficiency of certain units in particular and hospitals overall. From these results, we can conclude that Lean contains six principles:[5]

1. Lean is an attitude toward continuous improvement. It is characterized by the plan, do, study, act (PDSA) cycle.[6] It is actually similar to scientific methods, and health workers are familiar with strict scientific methods from their education. Therefore, the principles should be easy to implement in the hospital.

2. Lean means creating value. Throughout the book, we find that patients eventually become a source of assessors and become a party who benefits, whether they are involved or not in the implementation. In turn, the value that increased for the patients also increases the value for doctors, nurses, investors, managers, payers, and, finally, the community in general.

3. Lean is a unity of purpose. Unity of purpose is difficult to build in the hospital because each worker has different tasks. The presence of this work variation makes it difficult to find an overall picture built on cause and effect in conjunction with other work and, finally, a general objective hospital. Lean helps them to see this literally through the value stream map and process map. Furthermore, Lean builds a common goal which is recognized by all involved parties.

4. Lean appreciates working people. It is a culture that is different from the traditional culture, which is hierarchical. All parties do not look at their position in the organizational structure; they should cooperate and receive criticism and input from each other. Instead, the hierarchy formed is actually reversed, where the determinant is no longer the managers but the executive of the field, such as cleaning service or a new nurse.

5. Lean is visual. It is not abstract concepts such as strategic management but a concept that is made concrete, starting from the observation stage to the implementation stage. Information has always been the handle and visualized in the diagram, whiteboard, markers, and deeds.

6. Lean is flexible. Flexibility seems to be separated from Lean when we talk about standardization. Many of the works that are too flexible are not standardized, and Lean standardizes them. But it is necessary to note that this standard is made by the employees themselves, collectively, and run by them. Although the standard is binding, the employees can also make improvements. Of course, these

improvements cannot simply be done without consultation. This would violate the standardization agreement. Improvements must still rely on the scientific method in the PDSA cycle. Evidence must be collected, the solution is discussed, the solution is run, and, finally, it is checked whether the solutions appear to function. If the solution is better than the standard, the old standard will be revised to the new standard. Here is the flexibility layout of Lean.

By holding onto these principles, let us begin to do changes in hospitals in Indonesia. After this, we attach a form example that can be used by managers who strive to apply Lean implementation in their hospitals by identifying waste in their areas.

Lean Implementation in <Unit Name>
How can we increase/decrease <Issue> in <Unit Name>?

How can we increase/decrease <issue> in <Unit name>?		
When do you feel frustrated? How can we help you?		
When do you feel the delay in<issue>?		
Waste type	Explain the waste examples you observed	What are your ideas to eliminate or reduce the waste
1. Damage Re-work, extra work, because of the errors process beforehand.		
2. Motion Unnecessary motion and travel or too long, such as seeking barracks, too far distance, etc.		

3. Overproduction Providing services or processes more than they should or accelerate something more than required.		
4. Transportation of goods or services Unnecessary exchange or care. The distance between material and information that is too far.		
5. Unnecessary waiting time People wait for something or information to come, or vice versa, officers wait for people to come.		
6. Stock Information or objects, for example, patient or specimen, one who waits in queue.		
7. Process Excessive or unnecessary processes. Things we do that actually do not add any value and even add costs.		

Adapted from Hereford Hospitals Lean Improvement in Pathology Form

References

1. Womack, J., Jones, D. 2003. *Lean Thinking: Banish Waste and Create Wealth in Your Corporation*. 2nd Edition. New York: Free Press.
2. Ciarniene, R., Vienazindiene, M. 2012. Lean Manufacturing: Theory and Practice. *Economics and Management*, 17(2): 726–732.
3. Shah, R., Ward, P. 2007. Defining and Developing Measures of Lean Production. *Journal of Operations Management*, 25(4): 785–805.

4. Angelis, J., Johnson, M. 2010. Lean and Organisational Fit: Unbundling Implementation. *POMS 21st Annual Conference*, Vancouver, Canada, p. 3; Hopp, W.J., Spearman, M.L. 2004. To Pull or Not to Pull: What Is the Question? *Manufacturing and Service Operations Management*, 6(2): 133–148.
5. Toussaint, J.S., Berry, L.L. 2013. The Promise of Lean in Health Care. *Mayo Clinic Proceedings*, 88(1): 74–82.
6. Moen, R., Norman, C. Evolution of the PDCA Cycle. Retrieved from: http://pkpinc.com/files/NA01MoenNormanFullpaper.pdf. Accessed on January 6, 2014; Staats, B.R., Upton, D.M. 2011. Lean Knowledge Work. *Harvard Business Review*, 89(10): 100–110.

Index